Nations in the News
UNITED KINGDOM

Afghanistan

China

India

Iran

The Koreas

Mexico

Russia

Saudi Arabia

Syria

United Kingdom

Nations in the News
UNITED KINGDOM

BY Jennifer L. Rowan

MASON CREST
Philadelphia · Miami

Mason Crest
450 Parkway Drive, Suite D
Broomall, PA 19008
(866) MCP-BOOK (toll free)
www.masoncrest.com

Copyright © 2020 by Mason Crest, an imprint of National Highlights, Inc. All rights reserved. No part of this publication may be reproduced or transmitted in any form or by any means, electronic or mechanical, including photocopying, recording, taping, or any information storage and retrieval system, without permission in writing from the publisher.

Printed in the United States of America.

First printing
9 8 7 6 5 4 3 2 1

Series ISBN: 978-1-4222-4242-1
Hardcover ISBN: 978-1-4222-4252-0
ebook ISBN: 978-1-4222-7580-1

Cataloging-in-Publication Data is available on file
at the Library of Congress.

Developed and Produced by Print Matters Productions, Inc. (www.printmattersinc.com)

Cover and Interior Design by Tom Carling, Carling Design Inc.

QR CODES AND LINKS TO THIRD-PARTY CONTENT
You may gain access to certain third-party content ("third-party sites") by scanning and using the QR Codes that appear in this publication (the "QR Codes"). We do not operate or control in any respect any information, products, or services on such third-party sites linked to by us via the QR Codes included in this publication, and we assume no responsibility for any materials you may access using the QR Codes. Your use of the QR Codes may be subject to terms, limitations, or restrictions set forth in the applicable terms of use or otherwise established by the owners of the third-party sites. Our linking to such third-party sites via the QR Codes does not imply an endorsement or sponsorship of such third-party sites, or the information, products, or services offered on or through the third-party sites, nor does it imply an endorsement or sponsorship of this publication by the owners of such third-party sites.

Contents

Introduction 6
1 Security Issues 20
2 Government and Politics 38
3 Economy 54
4 Quality of Life 70
5 Society and Culture 86
Series Glossary of Key Terms 100
Chronology of Key Events 105
Further Reading & Internet Resources 107
Index 108
Author's Biography 111
Credits 112

KEY ICONS TO LOOK FOR

Words to Understand: These words with their easy-to-understand definitions will increase the reader's understanding of the text while building vocabulary skills.

Sidebars: This boxed material within the main text allows readers to build knowledge, gain insights, explore possibilities, and broaden their perspectives by weaving together additional information to provide realistic and holistic perspectives.

Educational Videos: Readers can view videos by scanning our QR codes, providing them with additional educational content to supplement the text.

Text-Dependent Questions: These questions send the reader back to the text for more careful attention to the evidence presented there.

Research Projects: Readers are pointed toward areas of further inquiry connected to each chapter. Suggestions are provided for projects that encourage deeper research and analysis.

Series Glossary of Key Terms: This back-of-the-book glossary contains terminology used throughout this series. Words found here increase the reader's ability to read and comprehend higher-level books and articles in this field.

Rochdale Town Hall in Greater Manchester, England.

United Kingdom at a Glance

Total Land Area	94,058 square miles
Climate	Temperate, with little change in temperatures between seasons; over 50 percent of days are overcast
Natural Resources	Iron ore, lead, zinc, tin, coal, natural gas, petroleum, gold, limestone, salt, clay, gypsum, chalk, potash, slate, silica sand, arable land
Land Use	Agricultural land: 71 percent (25.1 percent arable land, 0.2 percent permanent crops, 45.7 percent permanent pasture); forest: 11.9 percent; other: 17.1 percent
Urban Population	83.4 percent of total population
Major Urban Areas	London (9.046 million); Manchester (2.69 million); Birmingham (2.57 million); West Yorkshire (1.864 million); Glasgow (1.661 million); Southampton/Portsmouth (912,000)
Geography	Islands in Western Europe, including the island of Great Britain, the northern one-sixth of Ireland, and Rockall and Shetland Islands; northwest of France between the North Atlantic Ocean and the North Sea; terrain includes rugged hills in the west and northwest, some mountains in Scotland, rolling plains and level lands in the east and southeast

Introduction

The United Kingdom is a European nation northwest of France, made up of four **constituency countries** that occupy what are known as the British Isles: England, Wales, Scotland, and Northern Ireland. One of the oldest European countries in history, the nation grew from the consolidation of various Anglo-Saxon kingdoms to the nation it is today over the course of nine centuries.

The difference between the United Kingdom, Great Britain, and England.

Words to Understand

Brexit: A term used for the departure of the United Kingdom from the European Union.

Constituency country: A country that makes up part of a larger country or confederation.

Mercantilism: A historical economic theory that focuses on the trade of raw materials from a colony to the mother country, and of manufactured goods from the mother country to the colony, for the profit of the mother country.

Spanish Armada: The Spanish naval fleet sent to England in 1588 as part of an invasion attempt.

Once the dominant world superpower in terms of territory and military strength, the United Kingdom today holds a key position in world diplomacy and global economics. A member of the European Union (EU) since its first iteration in 1973, the nation's voters passed a referendum in 2016 to leave the EU in a move popularly known as **Brexit**. The referendum and ensuing negotiations with other member nations of the EU have prompted concern over the United Kingdom's economic and political future, as well as impacted the ties between its constituency countries.

Creation of a Kingdom

The civilized history of the British Isles began during the height of the Roman Empire, when Roman territories stretched all the way to the border between what is now England and Scotland and involved the subjugation of various Celts, tribal groups native to the British Isles and parts of what is now Northern France. After the fall of the Roman Empire, the British Isles fractured into territories and kingdoms under the control of various Anglo-Saxon lords. These lords next faced conquest by the Vikings and then the Danes.

Although citizens voted to leave the EU, Prime Minister Theresa May has faced harsh criticism, and many protests have erupted calling for a revote.

In 1066, a force of Normans from what is currently Northern France, under the command of William the Conqueror, defeated the ruling Danish king and took control of what is now England. For almost 200 years, English kings of Norman descent would rule with increasingly absolute power.

In 1215, a group of barons and high-ranking nobility forced King John to sign the Magna Carta, or "The Great Charter." Among other things, the Magna Carta established limits on the power of the monarch and created a council of lords to advise the king in the creation and enforcement of all laws. This, in a sense, was the first legislature in England and the early precursor to Parliament. Various acts of this Parliament whittled down the power of the king, until the English Bill of Rights established the supremacy of Parliament in government affairs in 1689.

During the Middle Ages, the Black Death, or bubonic plague, devastated England's population and sparked the dismantling of the feudal system. Cities like London grew in size and prominence, and as the Renaissance reached England in the 1500s, the economy of the country grew and diversified. Meanwhile, the lengthy Hundred Years' War, a series of wars with France, eventually resulted in a battle for control of the English throne between two powerful families, the Lancasters and Plantagenets. The so-called War of the Roses ended with the ascension of the first Tudor king.

The rule of the House of Tudor lasted from 1485 until 1602, and during that time, England underwent several changes in government and society. Art, science, and literature flourished, with such notable contributors as playwright William Shakespeare, and England's role in the Age of Exploration began in earnest. The first attempt at an English colony proved a failure, and the mystery of the Lost Colony of Roanoke continues to engage historians and archeologists.

King Henry VIII, having been denied by the pope a divorce from Queen Catherine of Aragon so that he could marry Anne Boleyn, split from the Catholic Church and established the Church of England. An act of Parliament made the monarch the head of the Anglican Church. An ideological battle between Roman Catholics and Protestants would tear the country apart for decades; Henry's oldest daughter, Mary I, herself a devout Catholic, reestablished Catholicism as the official religion of the realm. Elizabeth I reverted

This illustration depicts King John refusing to sign the Magna Carta. Eventually, he was forced to sign and compelled to follow the laws that gave rights to the people.

Elizabeth I is credited with reverting England to her father, Henry VIII's, Anglican Church during her reign.

England's official religion to the Anglican Church upon her ascension to the throne.

Rise of a World Power

Under Elizabeth's reign, England's status as a rising world power began. The defeat of the **Spanish Armada** in 1588 placed England in a position of prominence on the seas. Voyages of exploration and conquest continued, with the circumnavigation of the globe by Sir Francis Drake, and the creation of trading ports in India and the Far East brought new riches to the nation. By 1700, England controlled portions of northeast Canada and a swatch of land between the Atlantic coast and the Appalachian Mountains that became 13 valuable colonies and soon possessed the strongest navy in the world. The system of **mercantilism** that developed between England and its colonies further enriched the realm but also sowed the seeds of discontent among independent-minded colonists in America.

Closer to home, the ascension of James I to the throne of England after Elizabeth's death solidified English control of Scotland. Prior to 1602, English control and influence had already existed in Scotland, thanks to conquests in the 1500s. The Act of Union of 1707 established England, Wales, and Scotland as one realm, known as Great Britain. The union would not be easy—uprisings in the early 1700s by the Scots attempted to drive out English rule. The defeat of the Scottish clans at the Battle of Culloden in 1745 secured control of Scotland by the English once and for all. By this time, Ireland had also come under English control, and an Act of Union in 1801 created the United Kingdom from all the countries of the British Isles.

The Industrial Revolution began in England in the mid-1700s, itself a result of the previous Agricultural Revolution that gave birth to new methods of farming. Improved farming techniques increased food production, which in turn resulted in an increased population. Cottage industries, wherein people produced textile goods within their own homes, gave way to mechanized production of textiles in factories. People flocked from the countryside

Cotton machines made a difference in the textile industry during England's Industrial Revolution.

to the cities looking for work and opportunities as the Industrial Revolution spread. Britain's wealth and influence grew, but so did environmental degradation and social inequities that plagued the country into the 1900s.

The Sun Never Sets on the British Empire

Great Britain lost its most valuable colonial holdings after the American Revolution, but its fortunes would not be reversed. Through the late 1700s and 1800s, Britain sought to maintain its worldwide power through new imperialist moves. Australia came under British control in 1770, and the colony there grew through the early 1800s. Britain also expanded its power in India, taking direct control there in 1858, and establishing spheres of influence in parts of China. In 1884, Britain was party to the Partition of Africa at the Berlin Conference, gaining control of more than one-third of Africa's land.

Canada and several islands in the Caribbean remained under British control during this time. British lands stretched around the globe by the dawn of the twentieth century.

The World Wars and Beyond

The two world wars tested the United Kingdom's diplomatic and military might. During World War I, Britain joined on the side of the Allied Powers in response to threats against various allies in Europe. Its participation in the conflict brought soldiers from far-flung corners of the Empire, from Australia and New Zealand, Africa, and India, to fight alongside native British troops in France and the Middle East.

Nationalism sparked the desire for independence among Britain's African and Asian colonial holdings, even as the nation gained yet more territory through the British Mandate that included Syria, Iraq, and Palestine. From the early 1920s through the 1940s, residents of British colonies began to clamber for control of their own lands and governments. Further conflict festered in Palestine when British officials increased immigration of European Jews into the country and promised to someday establish a Jewish homeland.

World War II brought yet another test of Britain's resolve and might. As the Nazis swept across Europe, Prime Minister Neville Chamberlain attempted a policy of appeasement that ultimately failed to stop the advance of Hitler's ambitions of domination. After France fell, the United Kingdom became the sole member of the Allies able to counter the German army, bearing the brunt of the offensive until the United States entered the war in 1941. In the face of military losses and direct attacks during the long Battle of Britain, the United Kingdom attempted to maintain an attitude of calm resolve that carried through to the end of the war.

IN THE NEWS
The Lingering Effects of British Colonialism

The United Kingdom lost control of its last African holdings in 1976, but the effects of British colonialism in Africa are still evident today.

During the Age of Imperialism, Britain did not impose direct rule on its African colonies, choosing instead to work with local native leaders whenever possible. But the government viewed Africa through a lens similar to that of mercantilism, where the value of the colony existed to enrich the mother country. This included the exploitation of both natural resources and the lives and labor of African natives, as well as the plundering of African art. An 1897 expedition to the Kingdom of Benin resulted in the theft of hundreds of pieces of artwork; similar acts by British authorities, including Cecil Rhodes, also stripped Zimbabwe of many of its treasures.

Other effects of British rule in Africa include institutions like school systems and even language; in Nigeria, the official language is English. In many African countries where European imperialism was particularly strong, citizens often do not learn their own histories. Britain's participation in the African slave trade further impacts their societies today, because the slave trade was severely detrimental to the overall demographics of these nations.

In recent years, calls have gone out to the United Kingdom and other European nations for the return of cultural items and artwork to the African nations from which they were taken during the nineteenth century.

Soon after the defeat of Nazi Germany, the United Kingdom had to face a number of diplomatic challenges. First, the tentative alliance between the United States, the Soviet Union, and the United Kingdom unraveled as Soviet leader Josef Stalin claimed total control over East Germany and much of Eastern Europe behind what Churchill called an "iron curtain." Nationalist movements in India resulted in that country's independence in 1947. The establishment of Israel as a Jewish state by British authorities and the subsequent division of the Holy Land between Israelis and Palestinians brought unrest from which British leaders decided to essentially step away. Finally, over the course of the twentieth century's second half, British colonies in Africa began, one by one, to assert, fight for, and gain independence.

The United Kingdom Today

Although the British Empire crumbled through the loss of territory, the United Kingdom has maintained an important role in world affairs into the present day. As a founding member of both NATO and the United Nations, including a permanent seat on the UN Security Council, Great Britian engages in peacekeeping and security activities around the world. Economic ties to Europe strengthened when Britain joined the European Union, though it did not take on the use of the euro as currency, choosing instead to maintain its own banking and currency systems.

As the second decade of the twenty-first century draws to a close, the United Kingdom celebrates many achievements but also faces many challenges. Society has become more inclusive, but minority groups continue to struggle for acceptance in certain regions. Strife in other parts of the world has brought displaced persons and refugees to Britain's shores, straining housing, health care, and social support systems.

Relations among the four constituency countries have been strained at various points, from referendums for Scottish independence to unrest in Northern Ireland between republicans who wish to see a united Ireland and those who support membership in the United Kingdom. Even Britain's connections to the rest of Europe have become strained, as many citizens and leaders believe participation in the EU has caused Britain's economy to stagnate. At the end of 2018, the aftereffects of Brexit on the United Kingdom's diplomatic ties, economy, and society still remain to be seen.

Text-Dependent Questions

1. What factors account for the growth of the United Kingdom's role as a world power in the 1700s and 1800s?
2. What challenges have come about due to the influx of refugees into the United Kingdom?
3. What role(s) does the United Kingdom hold in the international community today?

Research Project

Choose an African country that was once a British colonial possession. Research the reasons for British colonization there and the realities of life in the chosen country under colonial rule. Write a four- to five-paragraph essay describing the pros and cons of British rule, including a determination of which country was most affected by each pro and con. Extension: Research and describe the ways in which British colonialism still influences that African nation today.

Introduction 17

After a 2016 referendum on whether to leave the European Union, Britain became mired in the details of how to extricate itself from the EU.

The United Kingdom in the News in the 21st Century

Risk of No-Deal Brexit 'Very High', Says Key EU Negotiator
Guardian, January 28, 2019

Theresa May Defies Tory Rebels to Press on with Brexit Deal
Guardian, November 19, 2018

Brexit Tension Leads UK to Seek Deeper Ties with Canada
CBC, October 6, 2018

Britain to Almost Double Troops in Afghanistan after U.S. Request
Reuters, July 10, 2018

UK Hospitals Are Overburdened, But the British Love Their Universal Health Care
NPR, March 7, 2018

Deadly Attack Near UK Parliament; Car Plows Victims on Westminster Bridge
New York Times, March 22, 2017

Letter from Africa: Lingering Cultural Colonialism
BBC, November 3, 2017

EU Referendum: Most London Boroughs Vote to Remain
BBC, June 24, 2016

"IRA" Claim Bomb Was to Kill British Soldier Visiting Belfast
Irish Times, October 17, 2015

Scotland Rejects Independence from United Kingdom
New York Times, September 18, 2014

CHAPTER 1
Security Issues

The United Kingdom has long been a key diplomatic, economic, and military player in world affairs. Much of its history includes internal strife as well as involvement in wars abroad, and since the advent of the twenty-first century, this remains the status quo in many ways. The United Kingdom today deals with ongoing tensions in Northern Ireland that have simmered under the surface for 20 years, the threat of international terrorism, and involvement in multiple NATO missions around the globe.

Words to Understand

Bilateral: Something that involves two nations or parties.

Coalition force: A force made up of military elements from nations that have created a temporary alliance for a specific purpose.

Commonwealth of Nations: An intergovernmental organization, made of 53 member states that are mostly former territories of the British Empire.

North Atlantic Treaty Organization (NATO): A military alliance of European and North American democratic nations that formed after World War II to strengthen diplomatic ties and counterbalance the Soviet Union and its own military alliance.

Taliban: A fundamentalist Sunni Muslim political movement currently engaged in an insurgency within Afghanistan.

The United Kingdom's military has been at the forefront of strife all around the world. British soldiers are pictured here celebrating the capture of German trenches in Belgium during World War I.

United Kingdom's Security Issues at a Glance

Military Size	232,900 total personnel
Military Service	16–33 years of age for voluntary military service (parental consent under 18); officers 17–28 years of age; UK citizenship required
Military Branches	Army, Royal Navy (includes Royal Marines), Royal Air Force
Military Spending	$48.4 billion USD (2017)
Illicit Drugs	8.5 percent of population, England, Scotland, and Wales; 9.5 percent of population, Northern Ireland (2016–2017)
Active Terrorist Groups (home-based)	Continuity Irish Republican Army (CIRA), New Irish Republican Army (NIRA); 14 terrorist groups identified in Northern Ireland
Active Terrorist Groups (international)	Islamic State of Iraq and Syria (ISIS); al-Qaeda; al Ghurabaa; National Action (neo-Nazi organization); 74 international terrorist groups identified by UK government

Conflicts

The United Kingdom has diplomatically and militarily participated in dozens of conflicts worldwide for decades. Currently, British personnel operate in over 80 different countries in roles as peacekeepers, members of **coalition forces**, or advisors.

British military involvement exists in parts of the Middle East and Central Asia. In the early 2000s, troops from the United Kingdom joined forces led by the United States in both the Afghanistan War that helped oust the **Taliban** regime in 2001, as well as the 2003 invasion of Iraq that led to the toppling of Saddam Hussein's dictatorship. British involvement in Iraq, in particular, drew criticism of then prime minister Tony Blair in that, despite U.S. involvement in the region, the conflict posed no serious threat to the United Kingdom. The prime minister's successor, Gordon Brown, ordered an inquiry in 2009. Blair staunchly defended his decision as late as 2016, stating that he acted on good faith over reports that Hussein held control of weapons of mass destruction and posed a threat to global security. He also posited that Brown's 2009 Iraq inquiry proved he had not misled the British people or manipulated intel-

British soldiers take part in a training exercise.

ligence, two accusations that were common as a British presence in Iraq grew more and more unpopular.

After combat operations ended in Afghanistan, a small force of 450 British soldiers remained through the end of 2015 to train and advise Afghan security forces. These troops were withdrawn from Afghanistan, but at the urging of U.S. President Donald Trump, Prime Minister Theresa May committed the return of over 400 British troops to Afghanistan in 2018 to aid U.S. forces still stationed there, a move that has drawn criticism. Britain's combat involvement in Iraq ended in 2009, with a small force remaining to train and advice Iraqi security forces. In July of 2015, then prime minister David Cameron authorized the deployment of over 120 troops back to Iraq in response to increased activity by the Islamic State.

Heightened tensions in the Baltic region that occurred after the Russian annexation of Crimea have resulted in the deployment of British military personnel to that region. The purpose of the UK presence is to provide some reassurance to Eastern European members of the **North Atlantic Treaty Organization (NATO)**. Here, British troops act as advisors and trainers for international

Military members rearm an AH 64 Longbow Apache attack helicopter in Afghanistan during Operation Herrick.

armed forces, and the Royal Air Force has provided assistance with air patrol operations.

Other operations worldwide that have involved British intervention include the fight against Boko Haram in Nigeria, as well as peacekeeping operations in Somalia and Kenya and naval operations near Bahrain. The United Kingdom has also been affected by the growing refugee crisis that began sweeping Europe in the early 2010s. By 2016, the United Kingdom had accepted almost 40,000 refugees from Syria, Iran, Afghanistan, and Pakistan, plus another 36,000 from Zimbabwe, Eritrea, Sudan, and Somalia.

IN THE NEWS
Chemical Weapons Attacks in Syria Prompt UK Action

Up until early 2018, the United Kingdom was not directly involved in the Syrian civil war, though it has provided support for moderate rebels. Then, for the second time in two years, chemical weapons were deployed in war-ravaged areas under the control of Syrian rebels, resulting in injury and death among civilians caught in the crossfire.

International leaders called out Syrian president Bashar al-Assad, and Russia blocked the United Nations from investigating the attacks. The United States threatened the use of air strikes against Assad in response, but the United Kingdom initially showed reluctance to determine what action should be taken.

A week after the chemical weapons attack, however, the United Kingdom, along with the United States and France, launched air strikes against supposed Syrian chemical weapons facilities. Prime Minister Theresa May addressed British participation in the air strikes to stress that the strikes had no goals beyond destroying chemical facilities controlled by Assad's regime, and that there was no alternative the three nations could take.

Russia, an ally of Assad, denounced the air strikes as an act of aggression.

Alliances

The United Kingdom participates in multiple international organizations and holds multilateral and **bilateral** alliances with many world nations.

Since its establishment after the end of World War II, the United Kingdom has served as a member of the UN Security Council. It is also a founding member of NATO and holds both political and economic ties to the various countries in the **Commonwealth of Nations**. The relationship between Canada and the United Kingdom is one of the strongest and most positive in the Commonwealth, because the two nations work together in areas of international development of health and education and global economic improvement. The United Kingdom is also a member of the Euro-Atlantic Partnership, the Organization for Security and Cooperation in Europe, the international forums the Group of 20 (G20) and Group of Eight (G8), the International Monetary Fund, the World Bank, and the Organization for Economic Cooperation and Development.

Regional Relations

In general, the relationship between the four constituency countries of the United Kingdom are positive. Although England, as the most populous country and the location of the capital city of London, tends to hold the most political sway in national matters, each section of the United Kingdom retains its own cultural and national identity.

Northern Ireland

The relationship between Northern Ireland and the rest of the United Kingdom, particularly England, has long been a rocky one. After Northern Ireland split away from the rest of Ireland in 1921 to remain part of the United Kingdom, a number of political parties and paramilitary groups continued to work for the reunification of Ireland, free from British control. For almost 30 years, beginning in the 1960s, a period called "The Troubles" brought violent clashes between Northern Irish paramilitary groups and British troops deployed to the county. The violence, in addition to its political roots, also stemmed from tensions between Protestants and Catholics.

UK Prime Minister Theresa May and Canadian Prime Minister Justin Trudeau.

Eventually "The Troubles" ended with a tenuous peace that included the establishment of the Northern Ireland Assembly, a decision-making body affecting Northern Irish citizens. This assembly includes individuals from all parts of the political spectrum. In the early 2010s, renewed tensions resulted in pockets of violent activities in areas where Protestants and Catholics lived in close proximity.

The border between Northern Ireland and the Republic of Ireland poses its own issues. Under participation in the EU, the border between the two countries remained open; tourists, workers, and goods could pass with relative ease. A Brexit deal that results in a "hard" border could, according to concerned analysts, result in a renewal of violence and political turmoil; a sizeable portion of Northern Irish still supports a split with the United Kingdom and a return to a unified Ireland.

Scotland

The relationship between Scotland and the rest of Great Britain has been one of turmoil, dating back centuries to the conquest of Scotland by English kings in the 1500s. While an Act of Union in 1707 officially tied Scotland to England and Wales, various uprisings (like the Jacobite rising of 1745) and political maneuverings have continually asserted the view of many Scots that their country should not be part of the United Kingdom at all.

More recently, a referendum on Scottish independence was held in 2014, though the measure did not pass. As with Northern Ireland, the final results of Brexit may have consequences for Scotland's relationship with the rest of the United Kingdom. Scotland has

The Scottish independence referendum.

benefited economically from being part of the EU. Renewed calls for an independence referendum surfaced after the 2016 Brexit vote, because the majority of Scots voted against leaving the EU.

International Relations

The United Kingdom has a unique relationship with the United States that dates back to the era of British colonization in North America. After the Second World War, the two countries formed a diplomatic bond that has resulted in cooperation in a number of military operations, foreign policy issues, and other global problems. The United States provides financial support for the International Fund for Ireland, which aims to develop economic opportunities in the counties along the border between Northern Ireland and the Republic of Ireland.

The relationship between the United Kingdom and the European Union has proven rocky. Though the United Kingdom joined the

Winston Churchill and Franklin D. Roosevelt on the deck of HMS *Prince of Wales*.

precursor to the European Union in 1973, recent years have shown growing concern among British leaders, CEOs of businesses, and segments of the population that continued participation in the European Union is not in the best interests of the United Kingdom. A 2016 referendum fell in favor of the United Kingdom's exit from the European Union, a move colloquially known as Brexit.

By late 2018, the details of how Britain would cut ties with the EU had been debated and agreed upon by Prime Minister Theresa May and the leaders of the other 27 EU member nations. The deal would need to be finalized by a vote in Parliament. May called off the scheduled vote on December 11, 2018, because she hoped to negotiate better terms with EU leaders, particularly in the case of how the border between the Republic of Ireland and Northern Ireland would be handled. Her actions prompted a call by Parliament's minority government leaders for a vote of no confidence, which would put May's position as prime minister in jeopardy and, should her whole government lose a no-confidence vote, trigger a new general election. May rescheduled a new vote on the Brexit deal for mid-January 2019, and Parliament rejected the deal. The EU subsequently extended the deadline to October 2019.

The status of the United Kingdom's claim on Gibraltar, a rocky promontory on the southern coast of the Iberian Peninsula that provides strategic control in the Mediterranean, has also been contentious. An agreement between the United Kingdom and Spain, forged in November 2018, states that, after Brexit is finalized, the two nations will negotiate directly with each other over the promontory's fate.

Human Trafficking

Human trafficking in the United Kingdom includes forced or compulsory labor, domestic servitude, organ harvesting, and sexual exploitation. Forced marriage and illegal adoption are also categorized as human trafficking, and special focus is given on the issue of human trafficking of children. Human trafficking is often part of organized crime and can also involve the sale or transport of illicit drugs.

Reports released for the second quarter of 2018 showed that the number of known human trafficking victims in the United Kingdom had increased by 2 percent from the first quarter of the

The Rock of Gibraltar.

year. In July of 2018, 150 child slave victims between the ages of two and 17 were identified in Wales, many originating from outside the United Kingdom.

The United Kingdom's National Crime Agency established its Modern Slavery Human Trafficking Unit (MSHTU) to address the growing problem of human trafficking and modern slavery in the United Kingdom. The unit coordinates with local police forces and governmental departments, as well as the UK's Border Force and Immigration Enforcement offices. A hotline has also been established to report suspicions of modern slavery or human trafficking, and the National Crime Agency is working to educate the public to recognize signs of human trafficking. The 2015 Modern Slavery Act also aims to impose harsher penalties on offenders and improve protections for victims.

Illicit Drugs

Nations in the News: **UNITED KINGDOM**

The United Kingdom is a producer of small amounts of synthetic drugs and the chemicals used to make them. Rates of illicit drug use are high—the United Kingdom is a destination country for heroin produced in Southwest Asia, cocaine from Latin America, and a variety of synthetic drugs. Money laundering also occurs within the United Kingdom as part of the illicit drug trade.

Drug use survey statistics for England and Wales released in 2018 showed an overall decrease in the use of most illicit drugs, but usage rates for drugs like heroin and cocaine showed an increasing trend, especially among young people ages 16 to 24. Approximately 9 percent of adults between the ages of 16 and 54 reported using an illicit drug between 2017 and 2018, and almost 20 percent of youths ages 16 to 24 reported using an illicit drug in that time frame. The most widely used drug for the past several years is cannabis.

In 2017, the government released a national strategy to counter illicit drug use. The strategy focuses on building the skills necessary for young people to resist risky behavior, a change from the educa-

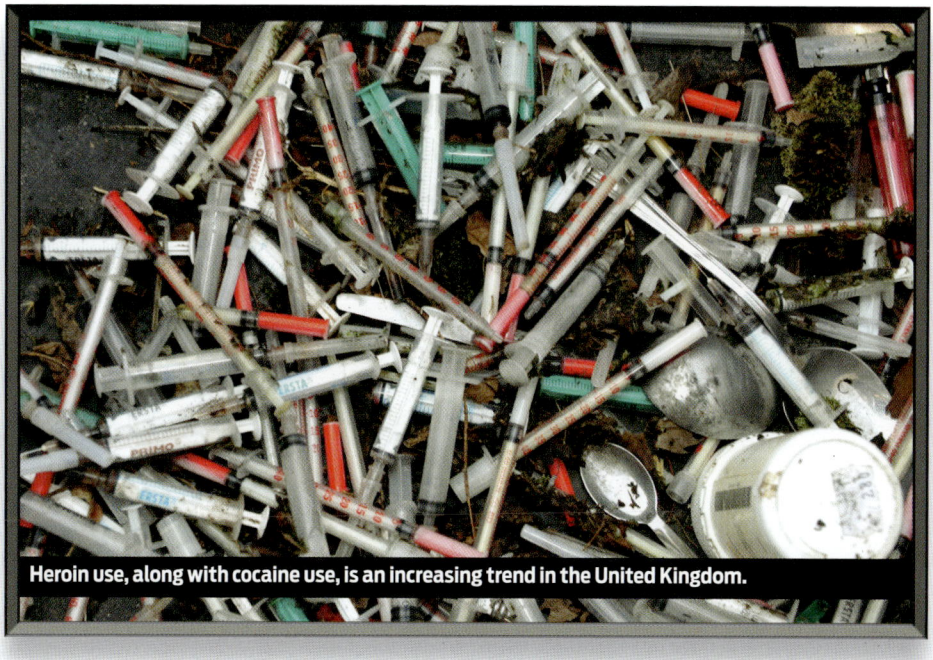

Heroin use, along with cocaine use, is an increasing trend in the United Kingdom.

Security Issues

tion-only strategies of previous years. Improved treatment is also a key element, as is addressing health and social inequalities faced by those with drug addiction and looking at how vulnerable adults, such as the homeless, can be provided with the services they need to tackle addiction.

Military

As of early 2018, the British Armed Forces numbered 232,900 total personnel. Of these, 150,250 were active duty, and 82,650 were reserve troops. Branches of the UK military include the Army, Royal Navy, and the Royal Air Force. The Royal Marines are part of the Royal Navy.

The Royal Navy was the world's strongest navy from the eighteenth through the twentieth centuries and remains the second largest naval among NATO member nations. The Royal Marines, an amphibious infantry force—meaning they are trained for battle on both water and land—is a division of the Royal Navy. The British Army was established when England and Scotland merged

A member of the Royal Navy takes part in a search-and-rescue training mission off the coast of Cornwall.

The Royal Air Force deploys their parachutes at an air show.

via the 1707 Act of Union and today is a key part of many United Nations peacekeeping forces. The Royal Air Force was established in 1918 and played a vital role in the defense of Britain during World War II.

Enlistment in the British Armed Forces is voluntary. Individuals must be citizens of the United Kingdom, a Commonwealth nation, or the Republic of Ireland, and be between the ages of 16 and 33; officers must be between the ages of 17 and 28. Parental consent is required for anyone wishing to enlist under the age of 18. Women serve in all branches of the military, including combat roles.

The Ministry of Defense oversees the operation of all branches of the British Armed Forces, and the mission of the military includes both foreign and domestic national security, as well as participation in coalition operations and NATO operations.

In addition to the British Armed Forces, each constituency country has a national police force. England and Wales have a police force of 128,000 personnel; Scotland's police force numbers 17,000 personnel; and Northern Ireland's has 7,200 personnel.

Members of Scotland's police force monitor crowds in Glasgow.

Terrorist Groups: Home-Based and Foreign-Based

The two major home-based terrorist organizations operating within the United Kingdom are the Continuity Irish Republican Army (CIRA) and the New Irish Republican Army (NIRA). Both are offshoots of the Irish Republican Army, a paramilitary group that works to end British rule in Northern Ireland and reunify Ireland as one country. Both are active in Northern Ireland, with CIRA operating primarily in Belfast and along the border with Ireland. Both engage in small-scale bombings and shootings; CIRA also engages in hijacking, extortion, and robberies.

Right-wing fascist groups also operate within the United Kingdom, and these groups often target blacks, South Asians, and members of the LGBTQ community.

International terrorist organizations have also plagued security in the United Kingdom for some time, with most instances connected to Islamic extremist groups like al-Qaeda and ISIS.

In 1984, the IRA bombed the Grand Brighton Hotel.

After the Manchester Arena bombing, a tribute filled with flowers and candles was set up at St. Ann's Square.

Six terror attacks occurred in 2017 alone, including a bombing at a London Underground station in September of that year and an attack on the Westminster Bridge when a lone attacker drove a vehicle into a pedestrian crowd outside the Parliament building. That same year, ISIS claimed responsibility for a suicide bombing at a concert hall in Manchester, and another vehicular attack and stabbings that occurred on London Bridge and at nearby Borough Market.

Over 120 people died in terrorist attacks in the United Kingdom between 2000 and 2017. The increased number of terror attacks has prompted the government to set the United Kingdom's threat level at "severe," although the overall number of fatalities in these types of attacks is down from what it was in the 1980s. British police work in conjunction with international agencies to investigate attacks and attempt to circumvent them with intelligence sharing, the securing of UK ports of entry, and other counterterrorism strategies.

Text-Dependent Questions

1. What prompted the United Kingdom to engage in air strikes in Syria in 2018?

2. What concerns have arisen over Irish border since the Brexit referendum in 2016?

3. What steps is the United Kingdom taking to address the issue of illicit drug use?

Research Project

Research the events that have occurred in Northern Ireland since the 1921 partition of Ireland, including British policies for governance, the political and paramilitary groups involved in "The Troubles," and the steps taken so far to maintain peace in the country. Acting as an advisor, prepare a three- to four-page report that contains the following: a brief overview of the history of conflict in Northern Ireland, the current status of political and social tensions, and an outline for action steps that Parliament and the Northern Ireland Assembly can take in concordance with each other to maintain peace and positive relationships between the constituency countries and the Republic of Ireland.

CHAPTER 2
Government and Politics

The establishment of the United Kingdom's government occurred over many centuries as the nation itself evolved. Once an absolute monarchy that included only the country of England, the government of the United Kingdom is now a parliamentary constitutional monarchy, in which the monarchs have become symbolic figureheads.

As a **commonwealth realm**, the United Kingdom includes not just the unified countries of England, Wales, Scotland, and Northern Ireland but also dependent areas around the world. These dependent areas encompass multiple Caribbean islands (Antigua and Barbuda, the Bahamas, Barbados, Grenada, Jamaica, Saint Kitts and Nevis, Saint Lucia, Saint Vincent, and the Grenadines), Belize, Canada, Australia, New Zealand, and parts of the South Pacific (Papua New Guinea, Tuvalu, and the Solomon Islands), as well as the promontory of Gibraltar on the southernmost tip of the Iberian Peninsula.

Words to Understand

Bicameral: Used to describe a legislative body with two chambers.

Commonwealth realm: A sovereign state in which the monarch of the United Kingdom is the reigning constitutional monarch.

Majority coalition: A cabinet of a parliamentary government in which several political parties cooperate to create a majority.

Peerage: A class of individuals holding a hereditary or honorary title.

Statute: A written law passed by a legislative body.

The Palace of Westminster is the meeting place of the House of Commons and the House of Lords—houses of the Parliament of the United Kingdom.

United Kingdom's Government and Legal System at a Glance

Establishment	December 6, 1921
National Holiday	None
National Symbol(s)	Lion (Britain); lion, Tudor rose, oak (England); lion, thistle, unicorn (Scotland); dragon, daffodil, leek (Wales); shamrock, flax (Northern Ireland); national colors of red, white, and blue
Constitution	Combination of statues and common law and practice
Legal System	Common law system with judicial review of Acts of Parliament
Voting Eligibility	18 years of age; universal

Constitution

The United Kingdom does not have a true written constitution in a form that would be familiar to most democracies today. Rather, it has what is referred to as an "uncodified constitution." Various iterations of written law have created a system of **statutes** that works hand in hand with the common law of England and Scotland.

Common law developed over a number of centuries, based on the principles of natural, or moral, law. It is based on precedent and, in many cases, legislated by acts of Parliament. The interpretation and implementation of common law can be changed via judicial review, thus reflecting the evolution of societal norms.

The Magna Carta (Great Charter of the Liberties of England), drawn up by English barons and signed by King John in 1215, is the founding document for England's constitution. The English Bill of Rights, passed in 1689, and the 1707 Acts of Union that established the union between England and Scotland further established principles that guided common law then, as well as today.

Acts of Parliament remain the source today for statutes and amendments. Either House of Parliament, the House of Commons or the House of Lords, may propose a bill for an act of Parliament. Any act thus proposed must be passed by both the House of Commons

The Magna Carta.

and the House of Lords, and the monarch must give royal assent. Recent additions include 2011's Parliamentary Voting System and Constituencies Act and the Fixed-Term Parliaments Act. The House of Lords Act, or the Expulsion and Suspension Act, passed in 2015.

Various international treaties and conventions impact British law and how citizens' rights and responsibilities are defined. The United Kingdom also must adhere to European law; the charter of the European Union, to which the United Kingdom is party, states that European law takes precedence over British law whenever the two systems are shown to be incompatible.

Establishment

The United Kingdom as it is known today was established in 1921 through the unification of England, Wales, Scotland, and Northern Ireland.

The growth of the United Kingdom occurred over many centuries. England, which also holds the nation's capital city of London, began as kingdoms united under one monarch in the tenth century. England and Wales united in 1284, and then followed acts of union that, by 1701, incorporated England, Wales, and Scotland as Great

Members of the Irish negotiation committee in Ireland.

Britain. The 1921 Anglo-Irish Treaty formalized the partition of Ireland, with the six counties that make up Northern Ireland joining with Great Britain to create the United Kingdom.

Legal System

Multiple systems of law operate in the United Kingdom: English law, English and Welsh law, and Northern Irish law. Scots law, a system based on civil law with elements left over from the High Middle Ages, is applicable only in Scotland.

The lack of unity in the legal system occurs due to the Treaty of Union, part of the 1707 Acts of Union that established the Kingdom of Great Britain. The treaty protected the ability for Scotland and Northern Ireland to have legal systems separate from that of England; to a degree, Wales holds a similar assurance. Certain laws apply to the entire United Kingdom, but rules of common law and equity, especially in regard to civil law, are where much of the legal system diverges among the four UK countries.

Political Parties

Twelve major political parties operate in the United Kingdom. These are

- Conservative and Unionist Party
- Labour Party
- Green Party of England and Wales
- UK Independence Party
- Alliance Party (Northern Ireland)
- Liberal Democrats
- Democratic Unionist Party (Northern Ireland)
- Party of Wales (Plaid Cymru)
- Scottish National Party
- Sinn Féin (Northern Ireland)
- Social Democratic and Labour Party
- Ulster Unionist Party (Northern Ireland)

For much of the late twentieth and early twenty-first centuries, the Labour Party dominated control of Parliament and the office of

Ramsay MacDonald was the first prime minister of the Labour Party.

the prime minister. The 2010s, however, have seen the growth of the Conservative and Unionist Party's dominance. The United Kingdom's current prime minister, Theresa May, gained that office in 2016 after the Conservative and Unionist Party became the **majority coalition** or party in Parliament.

Regional differences in political perspectives remain evident in the multiple parties representing the interests of Northern Ireland, Scotland, and Wales. Because the Labour Party and the Conservative and Unionist Party have dominated politics for decades, there is little opportunity for the other, smaller parties to sway governmental policies.

The Executive Branch

The fixture of a constitutional monarchy creates, in a way, two elements to the executive branch in the United Kingdom: the monarchy and the government, which is led by the prime minister's office.

The Monarchy

The ruling monarch holds the role of head of state; Queen Elizabeth II ascended the throne in 1952 and, in 2018, became the longest-reigning monarch in British history. The monarchy is hereditary, and various

Northern Ireland's Sinn Féin's current leaders, President Mary Lou McDonald and Vice President Michele O'Neill.

Queen Elizabeth II.

acts have established succession to the throne. Queen Elizabeth II named her son, Prince Charles, her heir apparent in 2018.

The monarch holds no real political or governmental power, however, and acts as a symbolic figurehead. He or she is tasked with appointing the prime minister from among the majority party in Parliament and presides yearly over the opening of the sessions of Parliament. The monarch signs new laws passed by Parliament, a requirement for a bill to become a law. The third major duty of the monarch is to meet with the prime minister once a week. At these meetings, the prime minister debriefs the monarch about governmental business and affairs of state, asking for opinions and advice. Despite having no political power beyond advising the prime minister, however, the monarch still retains full authority.

Members of the royal family have, for much of the past 50 years, devoted their focus and energy to various social and humanitarian causes around the world. The ruling sovereign also serves as the constitutional monarch for 15 of the Commonwealth countries.

Members of the royal family, like the Duchess of Cambridge, take part in various social and humanitarian causes around the world.

The Prime Minister

The prime minister of the United Kingdom acts as the head of government. The prime minister appoints members of his or her cabinet and other offices in the government and is responsible for the government's policy and decision-making process. Other duties include overseeing the operation of government agencies and the civil service, as well as acting as the principle government figure in the House of Commons. The prime minister also sets the agenda for the government, determines priorities for legislation, and decides which policies will be promoted in Parliament. As the acting head of government, the prime minister deals with foreign policy and guides the course of diplomacy with other world heads of state.

Theresa May became prime minister in July 2016 when her party, the Conservative and Unionist Party, gained majority status in Parliamentary elections.

Prime minister of the United Kingdom, Theresa May.

IN THE NEWS

Will Theresa May Face a Vote of No Confidence?

In the wake of a contentious vote on Brexit (the United Kingdom's referendum to leave the European Union), Prime Minster Theresa May faced a vote of no confidence at the close of 2018, after her controversial strategy for leaving the European Union prompted resignations among government officials.

Prime ministers are chosen from among the majority party after a parliamentary election, but if 15 percent of the members of the governing party lose confidence in their party leader, they may try to oust the sitting prime minister. These dissenting ministers of Parliament must submit written requests expressing no confidence, and if the required threshold is reached, a vote is triggered.

Voters across the United Kingdom cast ballots on the Brexit proposal in June 2016, and the referendum narrowly passed (most people in England voted in favor of the measure, although almost every voting district in Scotland voted to remain in the EU). Negotiations began soon after the referendum to determine exactly how the United Kingdom's exit would occur, and May's proposed strategy quickly drew ire from multiple sources over the transition period, citizens' rights, and payments to the EU.

If enough members of the Conservative and Union Party, the majority in Parliament, write letters of no confidence, May's future as prime minister would be cast into doubt. Another potential blow to the security of May's position is a withdrawal of support by the Democratic Unionist Party (DUP), a political party out of Northern Ireland that, to this point, has backed Conservatives and May's government. The loss of DUP's support would equal the loss of key votes that could otherwise save May's position. Should she be ousted by a vote of no confidence, the next step would bring the United Kingdom closer to new elections and, potentially, a new referendum on Brexit.

The Legislative Branch

In many ways, British Parliament's establishment dates back to 1215, when leading nobles forced King John I to sign the Magna Carta, securing the rights of certain members of the nobility to hold sway over the king's decisions. This early version of an English legislature gave way to the convention of the first elected Parliament in 1265. The **bicameral** Parliament formed in the 1300s, consisting of the upper House of Lords and the lower House of Commons.

A primer on Parliament.

For much of the six centuries that followed, the House of Lords remained the more powerful of the two houses. Parliamentary power slowly gained concentration in the House of Commons through the nineteenth century, eventually seeing a shift in prime ministers from the House of Lords to those chosen from the elected ministers in the House of Commons. Parliament confirmed the supremacy of the House of Commons in 1911, ultimately establishing the power of governance in this chamber.

The House of Lords

Seats in the House of Lords have historically been hereditary and reserved for members of the **peerage**. There are approximately 750 seats in the House of Lords (the number varies). Today, seats are held by 664 life peers (those ennobled for service to the nation), 90 hereditary peers from the United Kingdom's nobility, and 26 bishops of the Anglican Church. The monarch appoints members with advice from the prime minister and recommendation by the House of Lords Appointments Commission. The House of Lords Act of 1999 provided

Government and Politics

The House of Lords chamber sits in the Palace of Westminster.

for elections within the House to determine which hereditary peers would remain members, and new elections would be held only when vacancies occur among the hereditary peerage. No popular election is held to determine members of the House of Lords.

The main role of the House of Lords today is to discuss noncontroversial issues and evaluate projects that the House of Commons is unable to address. Beyond this, the House of Lords holds little parliamentary power. Although it can delay the passage of some bills proposed by the House of Commons, it cannot block bills. Delays are rare, and almost all bills are quickly approved and returned for a second look, often with suggested changes. Proposed changes are considered in the House of Commons for rejection or approval.

The House of Commons

The House of Commons, which essentially holds all Parliamentary power, has 650 seats, and ministers of Parliament are elected in single-seat constituencies by a simple majority vote. Unless the current House of Commons is dissolved, elections are held every five years. The last election for the House of Commons was held in July 2017, with the next scheduled for May 2022. The Conservative and Unionist Party won just over 42 percent of the popular vote in

Inside the House of Commons chamber.

the 2017 parliamentary elections, with the Labour Party coming in a close second at 40 percent of the vote.

The party or coalition of parties that holds a majority of seats in the House of Commons forms the government, and the prime minister is chosen from among the serving members of Parliament. Members of the government sit across the chamber from the leaders of the opposition (the party or coalition with the minority of seats in the House of Commons). An important feature of British Parliament is the role the opposition retains, via an official leader and what is termed a shadow cabinet, to table government ministers' bills and propose their own legislation. The opposition also has the ability to determine the agenda of the House of Commons. Debates in the House of Commons occur between ministers of the government and those of the opposition.

Motions by the opposition or private members' bills (those proposed by single members of the House of Commons) may be adopted if they are approved by the majority government. Typically, these proposals pass into law if they deal with a project that is of consensual concern or a noncontroversial nature, where ministers of Parliament vote according to moral convictions rather than party politics. An example of such a bill is the Murder Act of 1965, which abolished the death penalty.

The British Parliament acts as both the Parliament of England as well as the Parliament of the United Kingdom. Scotland, Wales, and Northern Ireland's regional parliaments or assemblies retain some powers as delegated by Parliament.

The Judicial Branch

The judiciary of the United Kingdom consists of a Supreme Court and various subordinate courts. Prior to the Constitutional Reform Act, passed in 2005 and implemented in 2009, the highest court in the United Kingdom was the Appellate Committee of the House of Lords. The Constitutional Reform Act established the Supreme Court as the highest court, replacing the Appellate Committee. Twelve justices sit on the bench of the Supreme Court, including a court president and deputy president. An independent committee of judicial commissions select candidates for justice positions; these individuals are then recommended to the prime minister and appointed by the monarch. Justices serve for life.

The different countries of the United Kingdom each have their own subordinate courts. In England and Wales, the Court of Appeal deals with civil and criminal cases. Other English and Welsh courts include the High Court and Crown Court. County and Magistrates' Courts also operate in England and Wales. Courts with similar names

Baroness Brenda Hale was named president of the Supreme Court in 2017.

and purposes are found in Northern Ireland, along with specialized tribunals. Scotland has a Court of Sessions, which handles civil cases, and the High Court of Justiciary, in charge of criminal cases. Smaller civil and criminal courts known as "sheriff courts," as well as various tribunals, also exist in Scotland. Examples of tribunals include an employment tribunal and an appeal tribunal, which deal with employment matters.

Overseas territories and dependencies have court systems under British rule, and some specialized courts in these territories include the Asylum and Immigration Tribunal and the Special Immigration Appeals Commission.

Legal advisers in the United Kingdom are divided into barristers and solicitors. Barristers largely focus on courtroom trials, whereas solicitors tend to draft legal documents, conduct negotiations, and provide advice. There has been more of an overlap between the duties of the two professions in recent years. Barristers and solicitors must be regulated and licensed to practice law.

Text-Dependent Questions

1. What elements, both current and historic, make up the uncodified constitution of the United Kingdom?
2. Why is the monarch of the United Kingdom considered a figurehead?
3. What factors prompted the possibility of a vote of no confidence on Theresa May's leadership in 2018?

Research Project

Choose three prime ministers who served in the past 100 years. Research each prime minister's government, policies, and political agendas. Write a five- to six-page essay comparing and contrasting the way each prime minister's actions and policies impacted the United Kingdom (government, economy, society). *Extension*: Create a visual presentation to illustrate the similarities and differences between each prime minister's policies and governments.

Government and Politics

CHAPTER 3
Economy

The United Kingdom is the tenth largest economy in the world, the third largest in Europe behind Germany and France, and maintains a role in the G7 (short for the Group of Seven, an informal **bloc** of industrialized democracies that meets annually to discuss common international issues related to economic governance, security, and energy policy) summit despite considerable debt. Financial services sectors have been a driving force behind the growth of the economy in the twenty-first century. The global recession of 2008 impacted the United Kingdom particularly hard due to the increasing economic impact of the financial sector, and the overall economy has been slow to recover. Further, the 2016 referendum vote to leave the European Union triggered a slowdown in the UK economy, because consumer confidence wavered due to warnings about the impact an exit from the EU would have on overall economic stability.

Words to Understand

Austerity: Governmental policies that include spending cuts, tax increases, or a combination of the two, with the aim of reducing budget deficits.

Bloc: A group of countries or parties with similar aims and purposes.

Briton: A citizen of Great Britain.

Nations in the News: UNITED KINGDOM

The 2018 G7 Summit.

United Kingdom's Economy at a Glance

Currency	Pound sterling (GBP); 2017 exchange rate: 0.7836 pounds per U.S. dollar
Labor Force	33.5 million (2017); 1.3 percent in agriculture, 15.2 percent in industry, 83.5 percent in services
Per Capita Income (PPP)	$44,300 (2017)
Inflation Rate	2.7 percent (2017)
Gross Domestic Product (GDP)	$2.628 trillion (2017)
Overall Unemployment	4.4 percent (2017)
Youth Unemployment (ages 15–24)	13 percent (2016)
Industries	Machine tools, electric power equipment, automation equipment, railroad equipment, shipbuilding, aircraft, motor vehicles and parts, electronics and communications equipment, metals, chemicals, coal, petroleum, paper and paper products, food processing, textiles, clothing, other consumer goods
Commodities	Manufactured goods, fuels, chemicals, food, beverages, tobacco
Imports	Computers, cars, gold, medicaments, foodstuffs, refined petroleum
Import Partners	Germany 13.7 percent, United States 9.5 percent, China 9.3 percent, the Netherlands 8 percent, France 5.4 percent, Belgium 5 percent (2017)
Exports	Cars, gold, gas, turbines, crude petroleum, medicaments, aircraft parts
Export Partners	United States 13.2 percent, Germany 10.5 percent, France 7.4 percent, the Netherlands 6.2 percent, Ireland 5.6 percent, China 4.8 percent, Switzerland 4.5 percent (2017)

Currency and Banking System

The currency of the United Kingdom is the British pound (GBP), or pound sterling. As of November 2018, the exchange rate stood at $1.29 (USD) to £1 GBP. One pound is made up of 100 pence (p), with coin denominations available in 1p, 2p, 5p, 10p, 20p, 50p, £1, and £2. Bank notes come in £5, £10, £20, and £50 denominations.

Scotland and Northern Ireland use the British pound as their currency, but the banknotes issued in these two countries are different from those issued in England and Wales. Scottish and Irish banknotes, while not given legal tender status in England and Wales, can be legally used in any part of the United Kingdom.

The Bank of England operates as the central bank of the United Kingdom and has operated since 1964. It is authorized to issue banknotes, holding a monopoly on this role in England and Wales while regulating the issue of banknotes by Scottish and Irish commercial banks. The Monetary Policy Committee manages monetary policy and must comply with orders from the Treasury department if extreme economic circumstances warrant them. Such orders must be endorsed by Parliament.

A handful of large banks, based out of London, dominate the UK banking system. These banks include the Lloyds Group, Barclays,

The currency of the United Kingdom is the British pound.

The Scottish banknote.

the Royal Bank of Scotland, and HSBC. Other banks operated on a wider scale prior to the global financial crisis of 2008 and 2009; in January of 2009, many banks began to consolidate in an effort to keep the banking sector stable. This consolidation also resulted in the need for tighter regulations to protect consumers and ensure stability and competition. In the United Kingdom, the Financial Conduct Authority ensures the fairness of financial markets.

Major U.S. banks and European banks dominate the investment sector, including such big names as Goldman Sachs, Morgan Stanley, and Merrill Lynch, though the largest UK-based banks have their own investment banking subsidiaries.

Labor Force

The United Kingdom has a labor force numbering 33.5 million people (as of 2017), with the percentage of the population's participation hovering around 79 percent from the middle of 2017 through the third quarter of 2018. Expert analysis of growth rates put the labor force participation rate at approximately 80 percent by the turn of 2019.

The majority of the labor force works in the services sector (83.5 percent), with another 15.2 percent working in industry. Automation and mechanization in agriculture has decreased the number of workers needed in that industry, and by the end of 2017, only 1.3 percent of the labor force worked in agriculture.

A 2017 analysis of information provided by the Office for National Statistics revealed that over 20 percent of the labor force in the United Kingdom is made up of migrants from the EU. These migrants' roles in the labor force are concentrated in sectors like fruit and vegetable processing, meat processing, the hotel and catering industries, and some specialist sectors like masonry.

Migrants have been able to come to the United Kingdom due to free movement that is part of the country's participation in the European Union. Potential migration restrictions that would occur once a Brexit deal is finalized have raised concerns about the future of migrants already living in the United Kingdom, as well as how vacancies, normally filled by such migrants, will impact the economic sectors that rely on their labor.

A group of construction workers repair a city street in London.

A woman holds a sign that reads, "Immigrants, we get the job done" at the March against Racism national demonstration in London.

Poverty

Poverty rates in the United Kingdom have risen through the second half of the 2010s, from 15 percent in 2013 to 20 percent by the end of 2017. A report by the independent Joseph Rowntree Foundation showed a total of 14.4 million people living below the poverty line. The population of children and pensioners (people who receive pensions after retirement) included in that total have, in the past five years, increased by almost 400,000 and 300,000, respectively.

The increase in the poverty rate is the result of various causes, among them a redefinition of the old poverty measure that placed the poverty line at 60 percent of the country's median household income. A new measure developed and implemented in 2018 sets a threshold of 55 percent of median total available resources—not simply what a family earns but also what it is able to spend in conjunction with the costs of living. Other factors include flatlined wages, rising costs of household essentials, and the impact of **austerity** budget cuts at the government level that have affected social programs.

IN THE NEWS
Brexit's Economic Fallout

Citizens across the United Kingdom cast ballots in June of 2016, voting on a referendum to leave the European Union. A hotly contested issue, the referendum passed, and negotiations began to iron out the details of when and how the United Kingdom would officially leave the EU.

Part of those negotiations, ongoing as of December 2018, deal with how various economic policies and trade agreements will be impacted. Under the terms of the treaty that created the EU, member nations enjoy free trade arrangements and the ability to move across borders with some ease, for the purpose of employment. At a microeconomic level, many have expressed concern over how Brexit will impact people's personal finances and households.

Although some economic forecasts predict the annual growth rate of the United Kingdom's gross domestic product (GDP) will improve, other indicators predict a drop in the GDP by 2020. Most parts of the economy will be affected, including income and wages, as well as investments and net trade.

Corporate and public perception of Brexit have been telling, especially as details of the UK-EU negotiations came to light. Almost 90 percent of chief financial officers and over 50 percent of small-business owners believe that businesses and the economy have benefitted from membership in the EU. The public has been divided on Brexit from the beginning, and public opinion continues to shift—in Scotland, for example, more than 68 percent of voters wanted to stay in the EU, and almost 15 percent of voters between the ages of 18 and 34 regret voting in favor of Brexit. Further, 40 percent of **Britons** expect Brexit to have a negative effect on the economy.

Even as the final details of the negotiations are underway, economic analysts cannot agree on the potential short- and long-term impacts. Concerns sharpened throughout the winter of 2018 over whether a deal would even be reached, and this prompted even more negative opinion among the British public about the Brexit deal at hand.

Poverty in the United Kingdom has continued to increase over the last decade.

The new measure identifies more specific groups that are disproportionately affected by poverty, including disabled people, single parents, and people without employment. Other studies have looked at the impact of poverty on children in the United Kingdom's poorest areas. In some constituencies, particularly those in poor urban areas, it is estimated that over 40 percent of children live below the poverty line (the average across the United Kingdom is at 27 percent), and these children are more likely to remain in poverty as they reach adulthood.

Agriculture

UK-based farming produces over 60 percent of the food and food products consumed within the United Kingdom itself. Major agricultural products include potatoes and other vegetables, sugar beets, cattle and sheep, poultry, fish, oilseed, fruits, and cereals, with wheat being the most widely produced crop in the United Kingdom. Other agricultural products related to livestock include dairy products and beef.

Approximately 71 percent of the United Kingdom's land is used for agriculture; arable land makes up a little over 25 percent of the

A combine harvester plows through wheat fields in Yorkshire.

agricultural land, with another 46 percent devoted to permanent pasture. Variations in climate and topography account for different types of farming found in different regions. Northwest England, Wales, and Scotland have land ideal for pasturing cattle and sheep, whereas the southwest portion of England contains pastural land for dairy cows. Croplands can be found in England's south and southeast, as well as the Scottish Lowlands.

With the looming conclusion of the Brexit deal, the Future Farming Consultation was launched in 2018 to determine agricultural policy post-Brexit. Growers, especially in agricultural industries that rely on export to the EU as well as labor from the EU, are concerned about how the United Kingdom's split from the European Union will affect them. Agriculture accounts for £24 billion in revenues and creates over 500,000 jobs between its direct labor force and those connected to other sectors of the economy.

Industries

Industry has long been a key aspect of the United Kingdom's economy, because England was the birthplace of the Industrial Revolution. Multiple factors combined to bring about the start of the Industrial

An Irish shepherd gathers his herd of sheep.

Revolution in the mid-1700s. Among these were an increase in population (itself a result of the Agricultural Revolution) that brought about higher demand for both jobs in growing industries as well as manufactured goods themselves; the development of central banks, stock markets, and companies that allowed people to invest in new technologies; and new manufacturing processes that increased and automated production.

Natural resources and geography, too, played a role. England was rich in coal and iron reserves, and the presence of navigable rivers and use of canals linked even interior manufacturing towns to ports on the coasts. It is often said that no location in England stands more than 75 miles from the coast in any direction.

The industrial landscape in the United Kingdom today is a mix of publicly and privately owned companies in a number of different sectors. Major industries include finance and banking, information technology, energy, construction, oil and gas, manufacturing, transportation and logistics, education, and wholesale and retail. The government and health-care systems are also major areas of employment.

Oil platforms are set in front of an incredible view in Cromarty—a small town in Scotland.

Mining once dominated much of the United Kingdom's economy. But as stocks of minerals become depleted, the industry has seen a shift from domestic production to the import of foreign minerals for processing in British facilities. Steel production is expected to experience stiff competition from foreign companies, potentially resulting in the reduction of workers.

Commodities

Commodity trading is a key aspect of the United Kingdom's economy. In 2017, the largest export commodities included machinery (especially mechanical machinery), paper, textiles, pharmaceutical products, and crude materials intended for manufacturing. Major commodity imports that same year included electrical machinery, mechanical machinery, and vehicles.

The pending Brexit deal with the EU at the end of 2018 cast the future of commodity trading into uncertainty. Physical and financial commodity markets work together to keep the United Kingdom's economy strong. Concern lies with how the deal will potentially

Cars like MINI, Honda, Toyota, Nissan, and Lotus can be made in the United Kingdom. The vehicles pictured here are ready for export.

limit the ability of UK exporters to ship goods to markets on the European continent, as well as the impact on consumers of commodity imports within the United Kingdom.

Imports and Exports

The United Kingdom exports goods to the United States and the European Union (particularly Germany, France, the Netherlands, and the Republic of Ireland), as well as to China and other nations worldwide. Major exports include crude petroleum, wheat, and precious metals like gold, silver, and platinum. Exports of precious metals have seen increases over the past five years, particularly for gold and silver, whereas the export market for British platinum has remained stable. Wheat production in the United Kingdom has increased by almost 23 percent since 2013.

Major import products of manufactured goods, machinery, refined fuels, and foodstuffs mostly come from the European Union, with significant imports also coming into the country from the United States and China. The United Kingdom is the fourth largest importer of goods in the world.

Through the end of 2018, the United Kingdom participated in free trade arrangements with the European Union member nations and the European Free Trade Association (EFTA). The United Kingdom is also a member of the World Trade Organization (WTO) and holds individual trade relationships with the United States, Canada, and Mexico, though not as part of the North American Free Trade Agreement (NAFTA) or the current United States-Mexico-Canada Agreement (USMCA). As a member of the EU, the United Kingdom benefits from free trade deals with 36 non-EU countries; questions have been raised about if and how those agreements will apply to the United Kingdom after the Brexit deal has been finalized.

Energy

By 2016, 100 percent of the United Kingdom's population had access to electricity. Over 55 percent of electricity comes from fossil fuels, another 9 percent from nuclear fuels, and almost 2 percent from hydroelectric plants. Other renewable sources, such as wind power and solar, continue to increase output; currently,

Inveruglas hydroelectric power station in Scotland.

Renewable energy in the United Kingdom.

renewable sources produce more than 20 percent of the United Kingdom's energy, and it is estimated that this will increase to 30 percent by the year 2020.

In itself, the energy sector acts as a major industry, thanks to reserves of oil, natural gas, and coal and the production of atomic power. International demand for fossil fuels has kept this sector

Economy 67

strong, though the coal industry has seen a drastic decline in the past 30 years. The United Kingdom exports energy to the European Union and other countries; as with other aspects of the economy, Brexit is expected to impact energy trade with the EU.

The Burbo Bank Offshore windfarm on the west coast of the United Kingdom in the Irish Sea.

Text-Dependent Questions

1. What actions were taken to stabilize the United Kingdom's banking and finance sector after the 2009 financial crisis?
2. How has the redefinition of the poverty line impacted the rate of poverty since the start of 2018?
3. How is the United Kingdom's energy sector changing in terms of energy sources and production?

Research Project

Research the economic agreements surrounding the United Kingdom's participation in and separation from the European Union, including impacts on trade, employment rates, prices, and wages since 1993. Then, acting as a spokesperson from the UK Treasury, write a report for Parliament outlining the pros and cons of leaving the EU as opposed to remaining part of the EU. *Extension*: Develop a visual (PowerPoint, infographic) to accompany your written report. The following article is a good starting point: https://www.bloomberg.com/news/articles/2018-11-19/u-k-treasury-to-compare-brexit-deal-costs-with-staying-in-eu.

Chapter 4: Quality of Life

In general, the United Kingdom provides a decent quality of life for its citizens and residents in terms of health care, education, and other basic needs, though that quality of life has stagnated in the past five years. Housing can be a challenge for many, and various impacts on the economy and the influx of migrants from Europe and other parts of the world have strained the ability of the UK government to implement stable policies and programs. If the country's population increases, resources diminish, and the economy slows as projected, issues faced by the populace may be exacerbated in the coming years. Quality of life for migrants is already significantly more challenging than for native Britons.

Basic Human Needs

When the basic human needs of a country's people are met, it results in access to other benefits that improve quality of life. Access to

Words to Understand

Apprenticeship: a training system in which someone works for an expert in a field or trade for the purpose of learning that trade.

Expat: Short for *expatriate*, a person who lives outside their native country.

Food security: The state of being able to access affordable, nutritious food in adequate quantities.

Neonatal: Of or relating to newborn children.

Potable: Used to describe water that safe to drink.

Nations in the News: 🇬🇧 **UNITED KINGDOM**

A woman begs for money on the streets of London.

United Kingdom's Quality of Life at a Glance

Life Expectancy at Birth	80.9 years (78.7 years for men, 83.2 years for women)
Maternal Mortality Rate	9 deaths/100,000 live births
Infant Mortality Rate	4.2 deaths/1,000 live births
Mother's Average Age at First Birth	28.5 years
Access to Contraception	84 percent of women (2008)
Physician Density	2.83/1,000 population
Prevalence of Obesity in Adults	27.8 percent (2016)
Improved Sanitation Facility Access	Urban: 99.1 percent of population; rural: 99.6 percent of population; total: 99.2 percent of population
Improved Drinking Water Source	100 percent of population
Electricity Access	100 percent of population
Telecommunications Access	Fixed line: 50 subscriptions per 100 people; cellular: 121 subscriptions per 100 people
Internet Access	94.8 percent of population
Broadcast Media	British Broadcasting Corporation (BBC), public service broadcaster; mix of public and commercial TV broadcasters over cable and satellite; national, regional, and local radio networks (via BBC); commercial radio stations; satellite radio services

medical care and **food security** are key to a stable life, as are clean water and adequate sanitation systems in promoting the overall health of the populace. The United Kingdom has a government-run public health-care system that ostensibly provides coverage and care to all residents. Certain groups experience inequitable access to care. Migrant populations and **expats** also tend to experience a lower quality of life; migrant and displaced persons in particular are susceptible to food insecurity, homelessness, and a lack of health care.

Nutrition and Basic Medical Care

The United Kingdom's health-care system is maintained and operated by the National Health Service (NHS), which is responsible for the public health-care sector of the country. All permanent residents are able to access public health-care, and coverage is free at the point of need and funded through general taxation. Eighteen percent of income tax goes toward health care. In 2017, the private health-care sector showed growth but remained small compared to the public sector. In addition to government-provided coverage, citizens also have the option to purchase private insurance.

The NHS has divisions that operate regionally in England, Scotland, Wales, and Northern Ireland. Gaps in coverage and care are currently being addressed by the NHS's long-term plans, with aims to improve care for older patients, shorten waiting times for

In 2018, people of the United Kingdom protested Health Secretary Jeremy Hunt and his policies.

appointments, and increase the number of hospitals and healthcare service providers. At present, wait times for basic medical care and nonemergency after-hours care are relatively short, but patients often wait longer to see specialists or to receive elective surgeries. In addition to Western forms of medicine, residents also have access to holistic and alternative medical treatments.

Food insecurity is an issue facing poor children and their families in the United Kingdom. In June of 2017, a report from the United Nations Children's Fund (UNICEF) showed that, at that time, 19 percent of British children under the age of 15 lived in families experiencing moderate or severe food insecurity. Ten percent of British children in this group face severe food insecurity, making the United Kingdom the worst-performing nation in the European Union for this problem. Another survey from early 2018 by the charity coalition End Hunger UK found that one-third of the poorest families in the nation skip meals due to an inability to afford food. Rising prices, national budget austerity that affects social welfare programs, and unemployment all factor into these rates.

Water and Sanitation

Access to clean water and effective waste sanitation is key to maintaining public health in any country. As of 2015, 100 percent of British households, both urban and rural, had access to clean, **potable** water. Additionally, over 99 percent of the population has access to sanitation facilities for waste removal. Prior to the 1980s, the availability of clean drinking water was threatened, often due to lapses or delays in the implementation of publicly desired environmental regulations. Government policies put into place since then to address the quality of inland water supplies righted the issue of freshwater access.

Shelter

According to a report by the Social Progress Index in 2017, only 44 percent of Britons feel they have access to affordable housing. On average, United Kingdom households spend about 24 percent of their disposable income on housing. As the costs of living rise, however, the ability of British families to maintain affordable housing is threatened. In 2014, analysts from the Joseph Rowntree Foundation reported a growing gap between the amount of money people needed to earn to cover the cost of rent or a mortgage and

Throughout the United Kingdom, men and women are hired to keep the streets clean. In addition, people may have access to public bathrooms.

their actual incomes. In London, housing costs can require up to half of a household's income.

Average rents in the United Kingdom can vary depending on if one lives in cities like London or the areas outside them. One-bedroom apartments in a city cost about $1,000 a month, while rent outside the city limits averages $850. Energy costs, municipal taxes, and other utilities add to the total housing bill.

Some cities, including London, are also experiencing a shortage of housing. In an effort to save space and money, developers have begun building what are termed "micro-flats," apartments that are around 250 square feet (23 sq m). Some younger adults feel this option provides a way to secure property, but opponents are concerned these micro-flat developments are creating slums.

Personal Safety

The United Kingdom is typically categorized as a safe country in which to live and travel. Street crime, such as muggings, tend to

A typical housing development in England.

More about micro-flats.

occur when a perpetrator sees an opportunity; residents and visitors are typically advised to remain in well-lit areas when walking at night and to be aware of one's surroundings.

The rate of violent crimes rose between September 2016 and September 2017. This includes a rise in knife crimes and murders, as well as sex offenses. A reduction in police personnel due to government budget constraints has appeared to exacerbate the problem of preventing violent crime, and some crimes go unreported.

The risk of terrorism is also high—the country has had its threat alert level set at "severe" since 2017. A number of high-profile attacks, many of them enacted by lone perpetrators that are part of Islamic extremist groups as well as far-right groups, have occurred in the United Kingdom. Among the most recent is the Parsons Green bombing that occurred in a London subway station in 2017 and

Quality of Life

Police officers on patrol in Bath.

Anti-terror police were on the scene after the bombing at the Parsons Green subway station.

injured 30 people. The Home Office, a governmental department in charge of national security, expects the threats from extremist groups to continue to rise. The department works closely with local law enforcement and national security and intelligence agencies to detect and deter attacks.

Personal Well-Being

Personal well-being is tied to living standards: The better a person's quality of life, the greater their sense of positive personal well-being. The OECD's Better Life Index reports that, overall, the United Kingdom ranks above average in education, environmental quality, social connections and civic engagement, and subjective well-being or personal happiness.

Education

On average, Britons in England and Wales can expect to complete 18 years of education. The education system is divided into primary education, secondary education, further education, and higher education. Children enter primary school at the age of five, and school attendance is compulsory until 16 years of age. Schools are either government-funded state schools or independent schools that charge tuition fees for attendance. All state schools in England and Wales must follow a national curriculum that was adopted in 1988. Independent schools do not have to follow the national curriculum, but they must prove yearly that they provide a well-rounded education.

Student progress is assessed when a child reaches the ages of seven, 11, 14, and 16. Assessments taken at age 16, at the end of secondary education, determine whether a student will move into further education and, potentially, higher education, or if they will

School children take part in an arts and crafts lesson.

enter the labor force. Students who plan to go to university must complete further education.

Scotland's education system operates separately from that of England. Scottish students enter early learning schools and childcare at age three and must attend through the third year of secondary school at age 14. From ages 15 to 18, students enter what is called the "senior phase," which prepares them for higher education, employment, and civic participation.

Information Access

The 2000 Freedom of Information Act established that all Britons have access to information held by public authorities. The act covers all recorded information held by authorities in England, Wales, and Northern Ireland, and United Kingdom authorities in Scotland. Members of the public may request information at any time, and authorities are required to publish certain pieces of information about their activities. The act is designed to create a government based on openness and mutual trust. Personal data and information held by health-care providers is protected by privacy laws.

Approximately 95 percent of the population has access to the Internet, with 40 out of every 100 residents accessing broadband services. The 2018 Internet Access Survey revealed a 1 percent increase in weekly Internet usage among adults, from 88 percent in 2017 to 89 percent, and 9 out of 10 households have some type of Internet access. Mobile phone and smartphone usage have also increased.

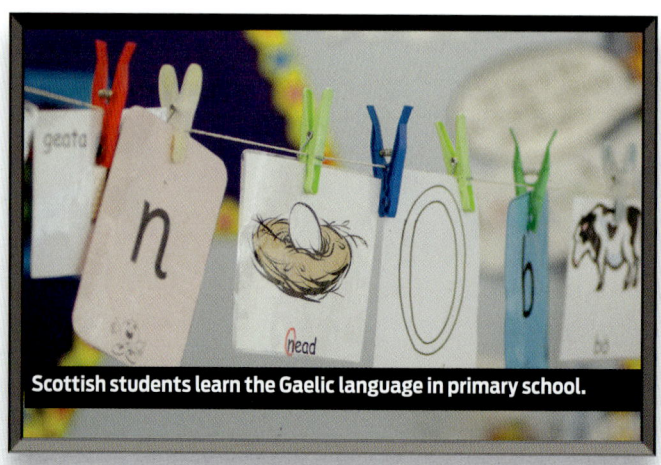

Scottish students learn the Gaelic language in primary school.

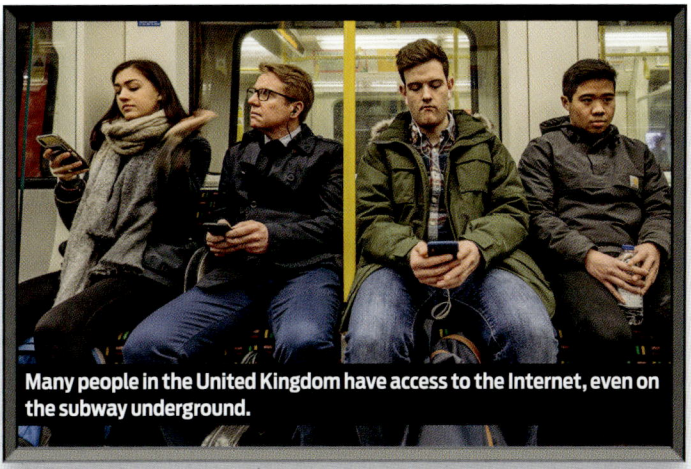
Many people in the United Kingdom have access to the Internet, even on the subway underground.

Broadcast media in the United Kingdom includes multiple television networks and radio stations operated by the British Broadcasting Corporation (BBC). Residents also have access to hundreds of international television stations through satellite and cable providers.

Health and Wellness

Policies and health programs in the United Kingdom have produced life expectancies of an average of 81 years, above the 80-year average found among countries that are part of the Organization for Economic Cooperation and Development (OECD). Women tend to have a higher life expectancy than men—83 years compared to about 79 years.

A 2018 study found that socioeconomic factors play a role in life expectancy, due to difficulties with accessing health care among the poor. Residents living in poverty die, on average, 10 years earlier than their wealthier countrymen and suffer higher instances of respiratory disease, heart disease, and lung and digestive cancers. **Neonatal** deaths and deaths in children under the age of five are also higher among the poor, and rates of dementia in older adults tend to be higher.

Additionally, a group of scientists at the University of Leeds have identified inequities in care between genders. One study found that women suffered a higher prevalence of death due to heart attacks than men because of unequal access to care.

BBC radio talk show host Jamie Owen conducts an interview.

Environment

Environmental pollution in the United Kingdom began with the onset of the Industrial Revolution in the mid-1700s. Long before environmental protections came into being, textile factories and manufacturing facilities produced large amounts of air and water pollution. Interactions with the British ecosystem, such as overgrazing, have resulted in poorly managed soils and reductions in productivity. Mountainous regions have been affected by the grazing of livestock, air pollution, and the effects of climate change, whereas other agricultural activities have created environmental issues in the lowlands. Climate change has also affected the environment, as it has in many parts of the world.

The government has enacted multiple policies aimed a reducing carbon emissions and conserving water. All companies must report carbon emissions annually, and environmental offenses hold higher penalties than in the past. The government has also supported the use of green technologies and the development of renewable energy sources by offering financial incentives to corporations.

Opportunity

Although economic inconsistencies have impacted the overall job market and earning potential of workers, almost three-quarters of people ages 15 to 64 have paid jobs. Training programs between colleges and local companies aim to build long-term relationships and strengthen the local workforce, with workers having the opportunity to become part of **apprenticeship** programs.

Personal and Political Rights

The government of the United Kingdom works to protect the civil liberties and political rights of its residents. Free elections and a free press are part of maintaining a stable representative government. Some governmental initiatives, however, have come under scrutiny over whether they infringe on people's rights, such as a move toward more surveillance of residents emails and other electronic communications by the Government Communication Headquarters. The surveillance program has been defended as a means to fight against organized crime and terrorism but has been met with criticism. Court cases have addressed the reach of two Investigatory Powers Acts from 2014 and 2016, and in 2018 judges found the program unlawful. The government announced plans to revise the law by spring of 2019.

In terms of political rights protected under British law, citizens have the right to vote in free and fair elections for their representatives in the House of Commons, as well as the ability to vote on referendums. Civil liberties include freedoms of expression and belief, which cover the press as well as protect access to the Internet, the right to assembly, and due process under the law.

Freedom of Choice

Residents of the United Kingdom ostensibly have freedom of choice, including the ability to move freely within the country, pursue

People enter a polling station to cast their vote on election day.

employment and educational opportunities, and live where they wish, provided the freedoms of others are not infringed upon. However, critics of various government policies and apparent social rigidity say that freedom of choice in the United Kingdom applies only to wealthy residents who can afford to live, work, and educate their children in the best parts of the country. Some see a holdover of a social class structure and colonialism that existed in previous centuries. Although there are no official policies that prevent social mobility between economic or social demographics, stigmas may still be perceived by some Britons based on their backgrounds.

Freedom of choice also extends to the health and reproductive rights of women. The 1967 Abortion Act legalized abortions in England, Scotland, and Wales. In Northern Ireland, abortions may be performed only in cases where the mother's life is at risk or the mother's mental or physical health would suffer permanent or serious damage should she carry a pregnancy to term. Any other instance of abortion in Northern Ireland comes with a sentence of life in prison, a penalty higher than any other European country.

Tolerance and Inclusion

Although the vast majority of native Britons are white (87 percent), the increasing number of minority residents has changed the face of the United Kingdom, both figuratively and literally, over the past several years. Schools have sought to provide better education on diversity and inclusion, while various organizations, like Tolerance International UK, works to provide programming for young people that is aimed at preventing and stopping discriminatory attitudes. Both universities and the government have provided suggestions and guidelines for more inclusive language, the most recent example being the advent of the spelling "womxn" instead of "women" to promote gender equity and acknowledge nonbinary individuals in certain university groups.

LGBTQ rights also vastly improved in the past 50 years, beginning with the decriminalization of homosexuality, in certain circumstances, in 1967 and, most recently, the legalization of gay marriage in 2014 (Northern Ireland does not allow gay marriage). Tolerance of the LGBTQ community and its rights has also increased, according to the 2016 British Social Attitudes survey.

Gloucester's pride parade.

Despite this, hate crimes targeting individuals of certain races and religions are on the rise; the rate of religious hate crimes in England and Wales went up 40 percent in 2018. The influx of refugees and migrants from non-European parts of the world have resulted in anti-immigrant and anti-Muslim sentiment. Hate crimes against members of the LGBTQ community are also on the rise, despite more liberal attitudes.

Higher Education

Upon reaching the age of 18, students in the United Kingdom may begin their higher education. They can pursue several higher education options: two-year diploma courses, bachelor's degrees, special foundation degrees for those looking to enter specific study areas like engineering or science, postgraduate degrees, and doctoral degrees.

The United Kingdom boasts some of the world's most prestigious universities, including

- University of Cambridge
- University of Oxford
- University College London (UCL)
- Imperial College London
- The University of Manchester
- The University of Bristol

Quality of Life

IN THE NEWS

Anti-Immigrant Sentiment Targets Children

Syrian refugees in the United Kingdom face a difficult social and political environment, and that environment has been described as increasingly toxic in the wake of rising anti-immigrant sentiment. The harsh reality of hate crimes and discrimination faced by these refugees was exposed in late November 2018, when a Syrian schoolboy faced a violent attack by classmates.

According to reports, a video depicted a 15-year-old boy being grabbed by the neck and thrown to the floor at his school. Though many hate crimes go unreported, 10 percent of those that are reported involve incidents in schools.

The Syria Solidarity Campaign's cofounder, Abdulaziz Almashi, reiterated that more and more Syrian refugees report experiencing hate crimes. In addition to the attack on the schoolboy, another report told of a Syrian girl in a hijab who was pushed in front of a train in London. A Scottish teen faces seven years in prison for the attempted murder of a Syrian refugee, and a refugee family fled their home in the middle of the night after an arson attack. Young Syrians also experience abusive language online that spills into daily life, fueling the bullying they experience.

- London School of Economics and Political Science (LSE)
- The University of Nottingham
- The University of Edinburgh
- King's College London (KCL)

In 2014, 580,000 students applied to begin their higher education, a 4 percent increase from the previous year. During the 2016 to 2017 academic year, approximately 2.32 million students were enrolled at colleges and universities in the United Kingdom. The year 2017 also saw an increase in the percent of students from low-income families attending university, from 11.2 percent in 2006 to 20.4 percent.

New College at Oxford University.

Text-Dependent Questions

1. How has the British government worked to improve basic medical care for UK residents?

2. Why has it become difficult for certain segments of the population to find affordable housing?

3. What are the challenges faced by minority groups and refugees in the United Kingdom in terms of tolerance and inclusion?

Research Project

Research the housing market in a major UK city, including estimated annual costs of rent/mortgage payments, taxes, and utilities. Then research different approaches to housing shortages (availability and/or costs). Prepare a four- to six-paragraph essay explaining the housing problems faced by that city and outlining two potential solutions to the problems.

Quality of Life

Chapter 5
Society and Culture

The United Kingdom exists as a unique entity, because four distinct countries (England, Scotland, Wales, and Northern Ireland) make up the nation. In terms of nationality, all citizens of the United Kingdom are internationally referred to as British, though many prefer to be referred to by their country of origin (English, Scottish, Welsh, and Irish, respectively). The cultural and societal variations in each of the constituent countries make it challenging to describe the nation as a whole, though some elements of society and culture are common across constituency borders.

As the current political climate leans toward conservativism, it is easy to view the overall temperament of Britons as conservative in themselves. Clothing, particularly in business settings, tends to be more formal than in other Western democracies, and formality of language and demeanor is also common.

Attitudes about family and marriage, once deeply ingrained in British culture, have changed in the past 50 years. Single-parent

Words to Understand

Bank holiday: A public holiday when banks and many other businesses are closed.

Celtic: A language group relating to the Celts, a branch of the Indo-European family, which includes Scottish Gaelic, Irish, Welsh, and Cornish.

Gaelic: The Celtic language of Scotland.

A group of businesspeople en route to work.

United Kingdom's Society and Culture at a Glance

Population	65,105,246 (July 2018 estimate); populations of constituent countries: England—55,268,100; Scotland—5,404,700; Wales—3,113,200; Northern Ireland—1,862,100
Sex Ratio	0.99 males/female
Age Distribution	17.59 percent age 0–14; 11.71 percent age 15–24; 40.29 percent age 25–54; 12.22 percent age 55–64; 18.19 percent age 65 and over
Ethnic Groups	White 87.2 percent; black/African/Caribbean/black British 3 percent; Asian/Asian British: Indian 2.3 percent; Asian/Asian British: Pakistani 1.9 percent; mixed 2 percent; other 3.7 percent
Religions	Christian, including Anglican, Roman Catholic, Presbyterian, Methodist 59.5 percent, Muslim 4.4 percent, Hindu 1.3 percent, other 2 percent, unspecified 7.2 percent, none 25.7 percent
Languages	English, Scottish Gaelic (about 60,000 in Scotland), Welsh (about 20 percent of the population of Wales), Irish (about 10 percent of the population of Northern Ireland), Cornish (some 2,000 to 3,000 people in Cornwall) (2012)

families and cohabiting couples have become more common, and LGBTQ couples now enjoy protections under the law to enter into civil partnerships. Traditional responsibilities remain important to British culture—many younger families make commitments to care for elderly relatives, and over half of the population lives near immediate and extended family members.

Birth and Death Rates

Estimates in 2018 placed the United Kingdom's birth rate at 12 births for every 1,000 people, and the death rate at 9.4 deaths for every 1,000 people. This has created a net increase in population, though the rate of population growth slowed by 2.6 percent in 2017. The overall birth rate, by the end of 2016, had already declined by over 38,000 births from 2012's peak totals. The death rate, conversely, increased by 1.7 percent in 2017.

Despite this, net gain in population plus increases in immigration means the size of the population (over 66 million) has grown to the point that overpopulation is a concern. Analysts have outline potential problems as the population ages, particularly when it comes to filling

A family walks the streets of London with their newborn children.

jobs in certain labor markets and generating enough government revenue to support an aging population. Other concerns include the fate of the United Kingdom's consumable natural resources and infrastructure needs like housing, schools, hospitals, and sufficient water supply.

Religions

Since its establishment by King Henry VIII in 1534, the Church of England, or the Anglican Church, has been the official religion of the United Kingdom. Approximately 30 percent of the population adheres to the Anglican church. Other major Christian denominations include Roman Catholicism (10 percent of the population) and other Protestant denominations like Presbyterian, Baptist, and Methodist. Certain Christian denominations are concentrated in specific areas of the nation. For example, the concentration of Roman Catholics is higher in Northern Ireland than in other parts of the United Kingdom. Although a high percentage of Scottish are also Roman Catholic, Presbyterianism, or the Church of Scotland, is the state religion of that country.

An inside look at St. Peter's Roman Catholic Church in Belfast.

Adherents of Islam accounted for 4.4 percent of the population on the 2011 government census, and Hinduism is practiced by 1.3 percent of the population. Other Eastern religions practiced on an even smaller scale include Buddhism and Sikhism. Judaism is also practiced by some Britons.

The importance of religion in people's lives has, in general, seen a decline, particularly among Anglicans. Although the Church of England once held a dominant role in British culture and society, its role diminished over the course of the twentieth century's second half, to the point where less than half of the population attended worship services or followed a religion at all. Information from the 2011 census points to approximately one-third of Britons having no religious affiliation.

Ethnic Groups

The United Kingdom, as a whole, is predominantly white, with over 87 percent of Britons identifying as such on the 2011 census. Other major ethnic groups include black British or Afro-Caribbean—people from the Caribbean and former British colonies who are able to trace their ancestry back to Africa—who make up about

A Muslim man preaches in London's Hyde Park.

3 percent of the population. Just over 2 percent of the population is part of the British Indian community, and another 1.9 percent are of Pakistani ancestry. These populations exist in the United Kingdom due to Britain's long imperialist hold on India from the mid-1700s through the late 1940s.

The United Kingdom, over time, has become more ethnically diverse. The percentage of white Britons has decreased over the course of 20 years (the percentage of white Britons in 1991 was close to 95 percent), and that decrease may be attributed to a number of factors. Immigration from places like China, Greece, and Turkey has brought additional nonnative ethnicities to the United Kingdom; further, intermarriage between ethnic groups has increased, creating a larger population of multiracial individuals (2 percent on the 2011 census).

Concentrations of ethnic diversity tend to exist in urban centers, such as London, where white Britons count for less than half of the local population. A 2014 study by the London-based research institute Policy Exchange found that, though the number of white Britons remained the same between 2004 and 2014, the ethnic

Many families have migrated from places like China, Greece, and Turkey to live in the United Kingdom.

Society and Culture

minority population doubled in that 10-year time frame. The authors of the study posit that, by the year 2050, ethnic minorities could constitute up to 30 percent of the United Kingdom's total population.

IN THE NEWS

Are Racial Tensions on the Rise in the United Kingdom?

As the ethnic makeup of the United Kingdom continues to diversify alongside increased awareness of the racism inherent in Western societies, various analysts have looked at the rise of ethnic tensions and racial inequality within the United Kingdom over the past decade.

British minorities have historically suffered from a lack of opportunity in education and, by extension, employment. But through the second half of the 2010s, the children of Britain's minority groups are increasingly outperforming white British children in school. Although not an isolated factor, this, combined with increasing numbers of nonwhite immigrants coming into the United Kingdom, seems to have spurred a rise in xenophobia and its oft-seen result—hate crimes.

In August 2011, riots in London and other large cities resulted in attacks on members of minority groups, including the murder of three Asian men in a car attack in Birmingham. The rate of reported racially motivated crimes in England and Wales increased by 57 percent in 2016, following the Brexit referendum vote, according to the Equality and Human Rights Commission (EHRC).

Systemic inequality is still seen in multiple areas of society. According to the EHRC's report, ethnic minorities are twice as likely to be unemployed as members of the white community, make up less than 6 percent of judges in England and Wales, and are more likely to receive harsher treatment in the criminal justice system. Black workers with university degrees earn almost 25 percent less than their white counterparts. The group has outlined several areas for the government to focus on improving, including better reporting and research, and to establish clearer targets for decreasing inequalities in the criminal justice, education, and employment systems.

Languages

English is the official language of the United Kingdom, and an estimated 95 percent of Britons speak only English. Outside of England, a number of regional **Celtic** languages are still spoken—about 60,000 people in Scotland speak Scottish **Gaelic,** 10 percent of the population of Northern Ireland speak Irish, and 20 percent of the population of Wales speak Welsh. Welsh is afforded the status of an official language within Wales. Approximately 2,000 to 3,000 people in Cornwall also speak Cornish. Additionally, Scots, a Germanic language based on Old English, is spoken by about 30 percent of the Scottish population, and a variation, Ulster Scots, is spoken in Northern Ireland.

For many decades, Celtic languages were suppressed in the British Isles. Movements to promote the continuation of these languages and increased interest in reviving them have resulted in a growing number of native speakers. The slow resurgence has occurred due to educational immersion in regions where Celtic languages were historically spoken, rather than through governmental support for

Throughout Ireland, it is common to see signs written in English and Irish Gaelic.

Society and Culture

their reestablishment. Speakers of Celtic languages are inherently bilingual in their regional language and English.

Up to 30 different dialects of English are spoken throughout the United Kingdom. In areas with large numbers of immigrants, community languages include Italian, Polish, Greek, Turkish, and Cantonese. South Asian languages include Bengali, Punjabi, Hindi, and Gujarati.

Foods

As with languages, food in the United Kingdom sees variations across regions and cultural groups. At its core, British cuisine has certain commonalities, such as a traditional preference for combining a protein (such as beef, pork, lamb, or chicken) with two types of vegetables and potatoes. Iconic British dishes include:

- English breakfast: eggs, bacon, sausages, grilled tomatoes, mushrooms, tea, and toast
- Pork pie: pork, pastry, and gelatin, served cold
- Fish and chips: battered and fried cod or haddock, served with french fries
- Haggis: Scottish sausage made from sheep's organs stuffed with oatmeal, onion, suet, and seasoning
- Bara brith bread (Welsh tea bread): tea bread made with spices and dried fruits, like currants and raisins, and brewed tea for flavor and moisture

A full English breakfast.

Pork pies.

A family enjoys fish and chips.

Society and Culture

Haggis.

Bara brith bread.

Tea is one of the United Kingdom's most popular beverages; the average Briton consumes three cups a day, and the entire country drinks almost 165 million cups daily. Tea's role in society began with the upper classes, but through the eighteenth century it became a part of the daily routine for all members of society. Afternoon tea today is served as a light meal that includes finger sandwiches and pastries.

The presence of growing minority populations has impacted cuisine across the United Kingdom. Indian foods, for example, have become increasingly popular, with curry counted among the nation's favorite dishes.

National Holidays

Due to the fact that the United Kingdom developed over time through a series of treaties and acts of union, there is no particular national holiday celebrated by Britons as a whole. However,

Tea time is a popular afternoon break.

Society and Culture

multiple holidays are observed throughout the year, either in conjunction with religious observances or public holidays, during which many businesses and nonessential government services are closed. Official public holidays are regulated by the Banking and Financial Dealings Act of 1971, which replaced an Act of Parliament regulating **bank holidays** from a century prior. If a public holiday falls on a weekend, it is observed on the following Monday.

Religious holidays in the United Kingdom cover the major feasts and observances celebrated by Christians, Muslims, Jews, and Hindus. Certain Christian holidays are bank holidays, though the holidays of religious minorities are noted only among their respective communities.

Bank holidays may be observed on a national level or locally in certain regions and constituent countries. Whit Monday (occurring on the Monday after Pentecost), Easter Monday, the first Monday in August, and Boxing Day are bank holidays in England and Wales. Additional bank holidays may be determined on a yearly basis to include spring bank holidays. In Scotland, New Year's Day, Good Friday, the first Mondays in May and August, and Christmas Day are bank holidays. Certain religious feast days are observed locally in Scotland, Wales, and Northern Ireland.

What is Boxing Day?

Text-Dependent Questions

1. How has immigration and an increasingly diverse population affected British society in the past several years?

2. What problems does the United Kingdom face due to its increasing overall population?

3. How is racial inequality manifesting itself in the United Kingdom?

Research Project

Research the factors impacting the birth and death rates in the United Kingdom, as well as the projected effects the increasing population may have on the nation's resources (natural, capital, and human). Prepare a six- to eight-paragraph advisory report for the prime minister and other ministers of Parliament. Briefly outline your findings, provide rationale for at two areas of concern the government should begin to address now, and suggest action steps for one of those areas of concern.

Series Glossary of Key Terms

Absolute monarchy: A form of government led by a single individual, usually called a king or a queen, who has control over all aspects of government and whose authority cannot be challenged.

Amendment: A change to a nation's constitution or political process, sometimes major and sometimes minor.

Arable: Describing land that is capable of being used for agriculture.

Asylum: When a nation grants protection to a refugee or immigrant who has been persecuted in his or her own country.

Austerity: Governmental policies that include spending cuts, tax increases, or a combination of the two, with the aim of reducing budget deficits.

Authoritarianism: Governmental structure in which all citizens must follow the commands of the reigning authority, with few or no rights of their own.

Autocracy: Ruling regime in which the leader has absolute power.

Bicameral: A legislative body structured into two branches or chambers.

Bilateral: Something that involves two nations or parties.

Bloc: A group of countries or parties with similar aims and purposes.

Cash crop: Agriculture meant to be sold directly for profit rather than consumed.

Central bank: A government-authorized bank whose purpose is to provide money to retail, commercial, investment, and other banks.

Cleric: A general term for a religious leader such as a priest or imam.

Coalition force: A force made up of military elements from nations that have created a temporary alliance for a specific purpose.

Colonization: The process of occupying land and controlling a native population.

Commodities: Raw products of agriculture or mining, such as corn or precious metals, that can be bought and sold on the market.

Communism: An economic and political system where all property is held in common; a form of government in which a one-party state controls the means of production and distribution of resources.

Conscription: Compulsory enlistment into state service, usually the military.

Constituency: A body of voters in a specific area who elect a representative to a legislative body.

Constitution: A written document or unwritten set of traditions that outline the powers, responsibilities, and limitations of a government.

Coup: A quick change in government leadership without a legal basis, most often by violent means.

De-escalation: Reduction or elimination of armed hostilities in a war zone, often directed by a cease-fire or truce.

Defector: A citizen who flees his or her country, often out of fear of oppression or punishment, to start a life in another country.

Demilitarized zone: An area where military personnel, installations, and related activities are prohibited.

Depose: The act of removing a head of government through force, intimidation, and/or manipulation.

Détente: An easing of hostility or strained relations, particularly between countries.

Developing nation: A nation that does not have the social or physical infrastructure necessary to provide a modern standard of living to its middle- and working-class population.

Diaspora: The members of a community that spread out into the wider world, sometimes assimilating to new cultures and sometimes retaining most or all of their original culture.

Diktat: An order from an authority given without popular approval.

Disenfranchise: To take away someone's rights.

Displaced persons: Persons who are forced to leave their home country or a region of their country due to war, persecution, or natural disasters.

Economic boom: A period of rapid economic and financial growth, resulting in greater wealth and more purchasing power.

Economic reserves: Currency, usually in the form of gold, used to support the paper money distributed through an economy, available to be used by a government when its own currency does not have enough value.

Edict: A proclamation by a person in authority that functions the same as a law.

Embargo: An official ban on trade.

Federation: A country formed by separate states with a central government that manages national and international affairs, but control over local matters is retained by individual states.

Food insecurity: Being without reliable access to nutritious food at an affordable price and in sufficient quantity.

Free-floating currency: A currency whose value is determined by the free market, changing according to supply and demand for that currency.

Fundamentalist: A political and/or religious ideology based explicitly on traditional orthodox concepts, with rejection of modern values.

Gross Domestic Product (GDP): The total value of goods and services a country produces in a given time frame.

Hegemony: Dominance of one nation over others.

Heretical: When someone's beliefs contradict an orthodox religion.

Indigenous: Referring to a person or group native to a particular place.

Industrialization: The transition from an agricultural economy to a manufacturing economy.

Inflation: A general increase in prices and a decrease in the purchasing value of money.

Insurgency: An organized movement aimed at overthrowing or destroying a government.

Islamist: A military or political organization that believes in the fundamentals of Islam as the guiding principle, rather than secular law; often used synonymously (although not always accurately) with Islamic terrorism.

Jihad: A struggle or exertion on behalf of Islam, sometimes through armed conflict.

Judiciary: A network of courts within a society and their relationship to each other.

Mercantilism: A historical economic theory that focuses on the trade of raw materials from a colony to the mother country, and of manufactured goods from the mother country to the colony, for the profit of the mother country.

Migrant: A person who moves from place to place, either by choice or due to warfare or other economic, political, or environmental crises.

Militia: A group of volunteer soldiers who do not fight with a military full-time.

Municipal elections: Elections held for office on the local level, such as town, city, or county.

Nationalize: When an industry or sector of the economy is totally owned and operated by the government.

Parliamentary: Governmental structure in which executive power is awarded to a cabinet of legislative body members, rather than elected by the people directly.

Paramilitary: Semimilitarized force, trained in tactics and organized by rank, but not officially part of a nation's formal military.

Patriarchy: A system of society or government in which power is held by men.

Police state: Nation in which the state closely monitors activity and harshly punishes any citizen thought to be critical of society or the government.

Populism: An approach to politics, often with authoritarian elements, that emphasizes the role of ordinary people in a society's government over that of an elite class.

Propagandist: A person who disseminates government-created communications, like TV shows and posters, that seek to directly influence and control a national audience to serve the needs of the government, sometimes employing outright falsehoods.

Proportional representation: An electoral system in which political parties gain seats in proportion to the number of votes cast for those seats.

Protectionist: Actions on behalf of a government to stem international trade in favor of helping domestic businesses and producers.

Reactionary: A person who opposes new social and economic ideas or reforms; a person who seeks a return to past forms of governance.

Referendum: A decision on a particular issue put up to a popular vote.

Refugee: A person who leaves his or her home nation, by force or by choice, to flee from war or oppression.

Reparations: Payments made to someone to make amends for wrongdoing.

Republicanism: A political philosophy of representative government in which citizens elect leaders to govern.

Rubber-stamp legislature: Legislative body with formal authority but little, if any, decision-making power and subordinate to another branch of government or political party leadership.

Sanctions: Political and/or economic punishments levied against another nation as punishment for wrongdoing.

Secretariat: A permanent administrative office or department, usually in government, and the staff of that office or department.

Sect: A subgroup of a major religion, with individual beliefs or philosophies that divide it from other subgroups of the religion.

Sovereignty: The ability of a country to rule itself.

Statute: A law created and passed by a legislative body.

Subsidies: Amounts of money that a government gives to a particular industry to help manage prices or promote social or economic policies.

Tariff: A tax or fee placed on imported or exported products.

Theocratic: Of or relating to a theocracy, a form of government that lays claim to God as the source and justification of its authority.

Totalitarian: A form of government where power is in the hands of a single person or group.

Trade deficit: The degree to which a country must buy more imports than it sells exports; can reflect economic problems as well as strong buying power.

Trade surplus: The degree to which a country can sell more exports than it purchases; can reflect economic strength as well as poor buying power.

Welfare state: A system where the government publically funds programs to ensure the health and well-being of its citizens.

Chronology of Key Events

900s CE	Anglo-Saxon kingdoms unite to form the Kingdom of England.
1066	William (the Conqueror) of Normandy invades England and is crowned king.
1085	The "Domesday Book," a survey of English lands, is compiled.
1120	Death of Henry I's only son throws England into a crisis of succession.
1154	Henry II, the first Plantagenet king, takes the throne and rules over England, most of Wales, and parts of Northern France.
1190	King Richard I (the Lionheart) joins the Third Crusade to end Islamic rule of Jerusalem and the Holy Land.
1199	King John takes the throne after the death of his brother, Richard I.
1215	English barons force King John to sign the Magna Carta.
1283	Edward I conquers Wales.
1296	Edward I invades Scotland.
1306	Robert Bruce crowned king of Scotland.
1337	Hundred Years' War with France begins.
1348	The bubonic plague (the Black Death) arrives in England; nearly half the population dies.
1381	The Peasants' Revolt begins as farm workers revolt over high taxes, an unpopular government, low wages, and restriction of movement.
1453	The Hundred Years' War ends.
1455	The War of the Roses begins as the houses of York and Lancaster vie for control of the throne.
1485	Henry VII becomes the first Tudor king; his marriage to Elizabeth of York ends the War of the Roses.
1497	John Cabot, sailing for England, discovers North America.
1533	Henry VIII divorces Catherine of Aragon in defiance of the Vatican and marries Anne Boleyn; Anne gives birth to Elizabeth.
1534	Act of Supremacy places Henry VIII at the head of the English church; Henry establishes the Church of England.
1536	Act of Union unifies England and Wales under the English legal system and makes English the official language of the government; Henry VIII conquers Ireland.
1553	Mary I becomes queen and restores Roman Catholicism to England.
1558	Elizabeth I becomes queen, repeals Catholic legislation in England, and reestablishes the supremacy of the Anglican Church.
1603	James VI of Scotland is crowned James I of England upon the death of Elizabeth I; this unites the kingdoms of England, Ireland, and Scotland under a single monarch.
1605	A group of conspirators plots to assassinate James I and blow up Parliament as part of the Gunpowder Plot.
1649	Execution of Charles I begins an 11-year republic, with Oliver Cromwell appointing himself "Lord Protector" in 1653.
1660	The monarchy is restored under Charles II.
1668	The Glorious Revolution establishes William of Orange as the reigning monarch and recognizes the supremacy of Parliament.
1689	The English Bill of Rights establishes that the monarch rules in partnership with Parliament.
1707	The Act of Union dissolves Scottish Parliament, unites Scotland and England, and officially creates the country of Great Britain.
1745	The Scottish uprising, led by "Bonnie Prince Charlie," begins in an attempt to reclaim the throne of Scotland from the English; the uprising ends a year later at the Battle of Culloden.
1756	The Seven Years' War with France, the European offshoot of the French and Indian War, begins.
1757	Britain takes control of the Indian province of Bengal.
1765	The passage of the controversial Stamp Act, a tax on American colonists to cover the debt incurred during the Seven Years' War, begins a decade of unrest between Britain and its 13 colonies.
1771	The first cotton mill opens, ushering in the rise of the Industrial Revolution in Great Britain.
1775	The American Revolution begins when British troops clash with colonial militia in Lexington and Concord, Massachusetts.

1781	British general Lord Cornwallis surrenders to General George Washington at Yorktown, Virginia; the 1783 Treaty of Paris recognizes American independence.
1787	The first fleet of British convicts sails to Australia.
1793	War begins with revolutionary France; British troops are sent to Haiti in an attempt to put down the rebellion of Toussaint L'Ouverture.
1798	The Society of United Irishmen rebel against British rule in Ireland.
1801	The Act of Union creates the United Kingdom, which unites Great Britain with Ireland; Irish parliament is dissolved.
1807	Britain abolishes the slave trade, an action 20 years in the making; slavery would not be abolished in the British Empire until 1838.
1815	The Duke of Wellington, at the head of the British Army, defeats Napoleon Bonaparte at the Battle of Waterloo.
1837	Victoria I assumes the throne.
1845	The four-year Irish Potato Famine prompts heavy migration of Irish people to Britain, the United States, and Canada; the actions and inactions of the British government exacerbate the natural disaster, and about one million people die by 1849.
1857	The Sepoy Mutiny ends the East India Company's control of India and ushers in 90 years of direct British rule.
1880	Education of all children under the age of 10 becomes compulsory.
1884	Britain participates in the Berlin Conference, formalizing territorial boundaries of European colonies in Africa.
1901	Victoria I dies at the age of 81.
1902	The Boer War between the British and Dutch settlers in South Africa ends in a British victory.
1908	London hosts the fourth modern Olympic Games.
1914	World War I begins; Britain declares war on Germany in response to the invasion of Belgium.
1918–19	The "Spanish flu" kills more than 200,000 people in Britain alone.
1920	Britain takes control over Mesopotamia and Palestine under the Mandate System.
1921	The Anglo-Irish Peace Treaty partitions Ireland into Northern Ireland, which will remain part of the United Kingdom, and the Irish Free State.
1922	The Irish Civil War erupts over the retention of Ireland as part of the British Empire; full independence for the Republic of Ireland will not occur until 1949.
1928	Women over the age of 21 gain the right to vote.
1939	Britain declares war on Germany due to the invasion of Poland, and World War II begins.
1945	World War II ends with an Allied victory.
1947	India gains its independence from Britain.
1950	British troops join the Korean War in support of U.S. forces.
1952	Elizabeth II becomes queen; as of 2018, she is the longest reigning monarch in British history.
1957	Ghana becomes the first British colony in Africa to gain its independence.
1972	British troops open fire on a group of protestors in Northern Ireland in what comes to be known as Bloody Sunday.
1973	The United Kingdom joins the European Economic Community, now known as the European Union.
1979	Margaret Thatcher becomes the first woman to serve as Britain's prime minister.
1992	The Channel Tunnel, or "Chunnel," opens, creating a rail link between London and Paris.
1994	Britain hands control of Hong Kong back to China after 150 years of rule.
1999	The Welsh National Assembly and Scottish Parliament are established.
2001	British troops join coalition forces, led by the United States, in an invasion of Afghanistan to oust the Taliban regime.
2003	British troops participate in the Second Gulf War in Iraq.
2016	UK voters narrowly pass a referendum for the country to leave the European Union.

Further Reading & Internet Resources

Books

Ainsley, Dominic J. *United Kingdom (European Countries Today)*. Broomhall, PA: Mason Crest, 2018. A comprehensive volume that addresses the history, culture, government, and economy of the United Kingdom and its constituency countries.

Gagne, Tammy. *United Kingdom (Evolution of Government and Politics)*. Hallandale, FL: Mitchell Lane Publishers, Inc., 2014. A volume that looks at the evolution of the United Kingdom's government and political system within the context of its history.

Garratt, Richard. *United Kingdom (Major Nations in a Global World: Tradition, Culture, and Daily Life)*. Broomhall, PA: Mason Crest, 2015. A comprehensive look at society and culture in the United Kingdom.

Lonely Planet. *Not for Parents: Great Britain: Everything You Ever Wanted to Know (Lonely Planet Kids)*. Melbourne, Australia: Lonely Planet, 2012. A collection of interesting facts and stories about Great Britain, tied in with visual elements and photographs.

Peal, Robert. *English History: People, Places, and Events That Built a Country (Collins Little Books)*. Glasgow, Scotland, UK: HarperCollins Publishers, 2018. A comprehensive guide to the history of England, from the 1066 Battle of Hastings to today, providing information on key people and events that shaped the country.

Web Sites

BBC: History for Kids. *http://www.bbc.co.uk/history/forkids/*. An informational Web site geared toward kids, with sections on history and each of the constituency countries.

The History Channel: *Great Britain. https://www.history.com/topics/british-history*. A Web site with articles and videos about Great Britain's history from its founding to today.

BBC.com: United Kingdom Country Profile. *https://www.bbc.com/news/world-europe-18023389*. A comprehensive guide to the United Kingdom, covering the economy, government, society, and historical events.

Nations Online Project: United Kingdom Country Profile. *https://www.nationsonline.org/oneworld/united_kingdom.htm*. A Web site with an overview of the United Kingdom, with sections on each constituency country.

Britannica: United Kingdom: History, Geography, Facts, & Points of Interest. *https://www.britannica.com/place/United-Kingdom*. An online encyclopedia article with information about the United Kingdom's geography, history, economy, government, and society.

Index

abortion, 82
Act of Union (1707), 12, 27, 32–34, 40–41, 105
Act of Union (1801), 12, 106
Acts of Parliament, 39–40
   See also legislative branch
Afghanistan War, 19–20, 22–23
Africa, 13–14, 16, 19, 24, 90–91, 106
age distribution, 87–89
Age of Exploration, 9, 11, 105
agriculture, 6, 12, 58, 62–63
al Ghurabaa, 21
alliances, 25
al-Qaeda, 21, 35
American Revolution, 13, 105–106
Anglican Church, 9, 11, 50, 87, 89–90, 105
Anglo-Irish Treaty, 41–42, 106
Anglo-Saxons, 7–8, 105
Asians, 87
attitudes, 82–83, 86, 88
Australia, 13, 38, 106

bank holidays, 86, 97–98
banking, 16, 56–57, 64
Banking and Financial Dealings Act, 98
Baptists, 89
Battle of Britain, 14
Battle of Culloden, 12, 105
Bengali (language), 94
Berlin Conference, 13, 106
Birmingham, 6
Black Death, 8
blacks, 87, 90–92
Blair, Tony, 22–23
Boko Haram, 24
Boleyn, Anne, 9, 105
Border Force and Immigration Enforcement, 30
Brexit, 7–8, 17–19, 27–29, 48, 60, 106
   See also economy
British Broadcasting Corporation (BBC), 71, 79–80
British Empire, 8, 11–15, 105–106
British Isles, 7–8, 12
British Mandate, 13, 106
British pound (GBP), 56
Brown, Gordon, 22–23

Cameron, David, 23
Canada, 11, 25–26, 38, 66
Cantonese (language), 94
Caribbean, 38, 90
Catherine of Aragon, Queen, 9, 105
Catholicism, 9, 25, 27, 87, 89
Celtic (language family), 86, 93–94
Celts, 8, 86

Chamberlain, Neville, 14
Charles, Prince of Wales, 46
children, 29–30, 59, 62, 73, 77, 79, 84
China, 13, 66, 91
Christianity, 98
   See also individual forms of Christianity
Church of England, 9, 11, 50, 87, 89–90, 105
Church of Scotland, 89
Churchill, Winston, 16, 28
climate, 6, 80
colonialism, 11–14, 19, 82, 105–106
commodities, 55, 65
common law, 39–40
Commonwealth of Nations, 15, 20, 25, 38, 46
compulsory labor, 29–30
conflicts, 22–23
   See also wars
Conservative and Unionist Party, 42, 44, 47–48, 50–51
constitution, 39–40
   See also Acts of Parliament; legal system
constitutional monarchy, 38, 40–41, 44–46
Constitutional Reform Act, 52
Continuity Irish Republican Army (CIRA), 21, 35
contraception, 71
Cornish (language), 86–87
courts, 52–53, 81
criminality, 29–32, 74–75, 83
criticism, 81–82
culture, 9, 86–98
currency, 16, 55–57

Danes, 8–9
Democratic Unionist Party (Northern Ireland), 42, 48
demographics, 70–71, 79–82, 86–94
discrimination, 35, 82–84, 92
diseases, 79
diversity, 82–84, 90–92

economy, 54–68, 72–74
education, 64, 77–78, 80, 82–85, 89, 92
elderly, 59, 79, 88
elections, 39, 48, 50, 60, 81
electricity, 66, 71
Elizabeth I, Queen, 9, 11–12, 105
Elizabeth II, Queen, 44–46, 106
employment, 55, 80, 92
energy, 64, 66–67
England, 7–9, 11–12, 25, 38, 41, 52
English (language), 14, 87, 93
English Bill of Rights, 8, 40, 105
environment, 80

108   Nations in the News:  UNITED KINGDOM

Equality and Human Rights Commission (EHRC), 92
establishment, 38–41
ethnic groups, 87–94
Euro-Atlantic Partnership, 25
European Free Trade Association (EFTA), 66
European Union (EU), 8, 16–17, 19, 27–29, 41, 48, 54, 58, 60, 106
executive branch, 44, 47–48
exports, 55, 65–66
extremism, 75–76
　See also terrorism

fertility rates, 71, 88
food, 62, 70, 72–73, 94–97
foreign relations, 28–29
France, 9, 14, 54, 66
Freedom of Information Act, 78
freedoms, 81–83

Gaelic (language), 86
geography, 6–7, 64
Germany, 54, 66
Gibraltar, 30, 38
government, 29, 38–53, 78, 81
Great Britain, 6–7, 12–13, 41–42
Greek (language), 94
gross domestic product (GDP), 55
Group of 7 (G7), 54
Group of 8 (G8), 25
Group of 20 (G20), 25
Gujarati (language), 94

hate crimes, 83–84, 92
health care, 16, 64, 70–73, 79, 82, 89
Henry VIII, King, 9, 11, 89, 105
Hindi (language), 94
Hinduism, 90, 98
history, 7–17, 27–28, 40–42, 49, 80, 89, 105–106
holidays, 86, 97–98
House of Commons, 39–41, 49–51, 81
House of Lords, 39–41, 49–50
House of Tudor, 9
housing, 16, 70, 72–75, 89
human trafficking, 29–30
Hundred Years' War, 9, 105

illegal drugs, 21, 29–32
immigration, 58–59, 70, 72, 82–84, 88, 90–91
imports, 55, 66
In the News, 14, 19, 24, 48, 60
India, 11, 13, 106
Indians, 87, 91, 94, 97
Industrial Revolution, 12–13, 63–64, 80, 105
industry, 55, 57–58, 63–68
inequality, 79, 82, 92
inflation, 55
International Monetary Fund, 25
Internet access, 71, 78–79, 81
Investigatory Powers Acts, 81

Iraq Wars, 22–23, 106
Irish (language), 86–87, 93
Islam, 83, 87, 90, 98
Islamic State of Iraq and Syria (ISIS), 21, 23, 35–36
Israel, 13, 16
Italian (language), 94

James I, King, 12
Jews, 13, 16
John, King of England, 9–10, 40, 49, 105
Joseph Rowntree Foundation, 59, 73–74
Judaism, 90, 98
judicial branch, 52–53, 81, 92
judicial review, 39–40

labor force, 55, 57–59, 80, 88–89
Labour Party, 42–44, 51
Lancasters, 9, 105
languages, 14, 86–87, 93–94
law enforcement, 29–32, 34–36, 75–76, 92
legal system, 39–42, 46, 52–53
　See also statutes
legislative branch, 49–52
LGBTQ community, 35, 82–83, 88
life expectancy, 71, 79
London, 6, 9, 25, 41, 74, 91

MacDonald, Ramsay, 43
Magna Carta, 9–10, 40, 49, 105
Manchester, 6
manufacturing, 64
marriage, 82, 86, 88, 91
Mary I, Queen, 9, 105
May, Theresa, 8, 19, 23–24, 26, 29, 44, 47–48
McDonald, Mary Lou, 44
media, 71, 79–80
mercantilism, 11–14
Methodism, 87, 89
Middle East, 13, 22
military, 21–24, 32–34
mining, 65
minorities, 82–84, 90–92, 97
Modern Slavery Act (2015), 30
Modern Slavery Human Trafficking Unit (MSHTU), 30
monarchy, 38, 40–41, 44–46
Monetary Policy Committee, 56
money laundering, 31
mortality rates, 71, 88

National Action, 21
National Crime Agency, 30
National Health Service, 72–73
nationalism, 13, 16
natural resources, 6, 55, 64–68, 89
Nazi Germany, 14, 16
New Irish Republican Army (NIRA), 21, 35
Nigeria, 14, 24
nobility, 49–50
　See also peers

Index 109

North American colonies, 11–12, 28, 105–106
North Atlantic Treaty Organization (NATO), 16, 20, 23, 25
Northern Ireland, 6–7, 16, 19–21, 25, 27–29, 35, 38, 42, 44, 53
nutrition, 70, 72, 94–97

obesity, 71
O'Neill, Michele, 44
Organization for Economic Cooperation and Development (OECD), 25, 77, 79
Organization for Security and Cooperation in Europe, 25
Oxford University, 83, 85

Pakistanis, 87, 91, 94
Palestinians, 13, 16
Parliament, 8, 29, 39–40, 46–52
peers, 38, 49–50
per capita income (PPP), 55, 59, 73–74
Plantagenets, 9, 105
police. *See* law enforcement
Polish (language), 94
political parties, 42
politics, 25–27, 29, 38–53, 81
pollution, 80
population, 6, 87–92
poverty, 59–62, 71–73, 79
Presbyterianism, 87, 89
prime minister, 8, 19, 22–23, 26, 29, 43–44, 46–51
Protestantism, 9, 25, 27
Punjabi (language), 94

QR Video
 Boxing Day, 98
 England, Great Britain, and UK, 7
 micro-flats, 75
 Parliament, 49
 renewable energy, 67
 Scottish independence referendum, 19
quality of life, 70–85

racism, 35, 83–84, 92
refugees, 16, 24, 83–84
regional relations, 25, 27
religion, 9, 25, 27, 87, 89–90, 98
renewable energy, 66–68, 80
Republic of Ireland, 12, 25, 28–29, 35, 66
Rhodes, Cecil, 14
rights, 81–83
Roanoke Colony, 9
Roman Empire, 8
Roosevelt, Franklin D., 28
royal family, 44–46
Russia, 23–24

safety, 74–75, 83–84, 92
sanitation, 71, 73–74

Scotland, 6–8, 12, 16, 19, 27–28, 38, 41–42, 44, 53
Scots (language), 93
Scottish Gaelic (language), 86–87, 93
Scottish independence, 16, 19, 27–28
security activities, 16, 19, 22–24
Security Council, 25
 See also United Nations (UN)
sex ratio, 87
sexual exploitation, 29
Shakespeare, William, 9
Sikhism, 90
Sinn Féin (Northern Ireland), 42, 44
slavery, 14
 See also compulsory labor
Social Progress Index, 73
society, 86–98
socioeconomic mobility, 80–82, 92
Spain, 7, 11, 29
spending, 21
statutes, 40–41
Supreme Court, 52
Syria, 24, 84

Taliban, 20, 22
terrorism, 19–22, 24–25, 35–36, 75–76, 81
Thatcher, Margaret, 106
"The Troubles," 25, 27
tolerance, 82–83
trade, 55, 66
treaties, 41–42
Treaty of Union, 42
Turkish (language), 94

Ulster Scots (language), 93
unemployment, 55
United Kingdom (UK), 7, 12, 38–42, 86
United Nations Children's Fund (UNICEF), 73
United Nations (UN), 16, 24–25
United States (US), 14, 16, 23, 28
university, 78, 80, 82–85

Vikings, 8–9
voting, 39, 41, 81

Wales, 7, 12, 30, 38, 41–42, 44, 52
War of the Roses, 9, 105
wars, 9, 13, 22
 See also individually identified battles and wars
water, 71, 73, 89
Welsh (language), 86–87, 93
Westminster Palace, 39, 50
whites, 83, 87–92
William the Conqueror, 9, 105
World Bank, 25
World Trade Organization (WTO), 66
World War I, 13, 21, 106
World War II, 14–16, 28, 106

youths, 31–32, 55, 74, 82–84

Author's Biography

Jennifer L. Rowan teaches secondary social studies for Charlotte-Mecklenburg Schools in Charlotte, North Carolina. She holds two master's degrees, including a master of science in literacy education, and has over 12 years of teaching experience in New York and North Carolina. She is also a freelance writer and editor and an author of fiction. A native of upstate New York, near Syracuse, she now lives in the greater Charlotte area with her family.

Credits

Cover

Top (left to right): Morsa Images/iStock; Chris Strickland/iStock; GenoEJSajko/iStock
Middle (left to right): umdash9/iStock; oversnap/iStock; georgeclerk/iStock
Bottom (left to right): kylieellway/iStock; mbbirdy/iStock; dynasoar/iStock

Interior

1, Alexey Fedorenko/Shutterstock; 6, Alastair Wallace/Shutterstock; 8, Ms Jane Campbell/Shutterstock; 10, Everett Historical/Shutterstock; 11, Everett - Art/Shutterstock; 12, Everett Historical/Shutterstock; 15, Wikimedia Commons; 18, vasara/Shutterstock; 21, Everett Historical/Shutterstock; 22, Kevin Day/Shutterstock; 23, Rob Leyland/Shutterstock; 26, Bart Lenoir/Shutterstock; 28, US Navy/Wikimedia Commons; 30, Hellen8/Dreamstime; 31, Rainer Klotz/Dreamstime; 32, sam-whitfield1/Shutterstock; 33, Steve Meese/Shutterstock; 34, theasis/iStock; 35, D4444n/Wikimedia Commons; 36, Tomasz "odder" Kozlowski/Wikimedia Commons; 39, Offcaania/Shutterstock; 40, Earthsound/Wikimedia Commons; 41, National Library of Ireland on The Commons/Wikimedia Commons; 43, Bain News Service/Wikimedia Commons; 44, Sinn Fein/Wikimedia Commons; 45, Speedfighter17/Dreamstime; 46, Andrew Bartlett/Dreamstime; 47, Ojen/Dreamstime; 50, UK government/Wikimedia Commons; 51, UK government/Wikimedia Commons; 52, Dinendra Haria/i-Images / Polaris/Newscom; 55, Official White House Photo by Shealah Craighead; 56, Pigprox/Dreamstime; 57, Route66/Shutterstock; 58, Anton Havelaar/Shutterstock; 59, John Gomez/Dreamstime; 61, Roger Utting Photography/iStock; 62, Steve Allen/Shutterstock; 63, Marc Dufresne/iStock; 64, ZRyzner/Shutterstock; 65, Joel Carillet/iStock; 67, ATGImages/Shutterstock; 68, Ian Mantel/Wikimedia Commons; 71, Paolo Paradiso/iStock; 72, janecampbell21/iStock; 74, Caron Badkin/Shutterstock; 75, I Wei Huang/Shutterstock; 76 (UP), 1000words/Dreamstime; 76 (LO), Brian Minkoff/Shutterstock; 77, Brett Critchley/Dreamstime; 78, Carol_Ann_Peacock/iStock; 79, carstenbrandt/iStock; 80, AmandaLewis/iStock; 81, Daniel Heighton/iStock; 83, Peter Llewellyn/iStock; 85, pejft/iStock; 87, IR Stone/Shutterstock; 88, Massimo Parisi/Shutterstock; 89, Attila Jandi/Dreamstime; 90, funky-data/iStock; 91, NewStreetPhoto/iStock; 93, Helioscribe/Shutterstock; 94, Kevin Brown/Dreamstime; 95 (UP), Ben Gingell/Shutterstock; 95 (LO), Caron Badkin/Shutterstock; 96 (UP), Attila JANDI/Shutterstock; 96 (LO), D. Pimborough/Shutterstock; 97, kodachrome25/iStock